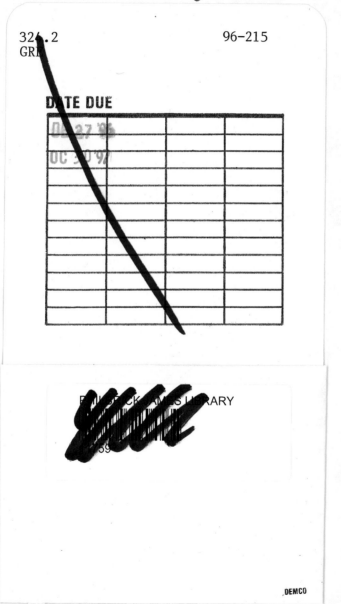

BIRTH OF THE REPUBLICAN PARTY

A Summary
of
Historical Research
on
Amos Tuck
and the
Birthplace of the Republican Party
at Exeter, New Hampshire

Compiled by Hugh Gregg and Georgi Hippauf

Resources of New Hampshire, Inc. Publisher • 1995

BIRTH OF THE REPUBLICAN PARTY

Resources of New Hampshire, Inc., 1995
Includes index
ISBN 0-9637615-1-X : $21.95
Library of Congress Catalog Card Number: 95-92284

Copies available from:

Resources of New Hampshire, Inc.
20 Gregg Road
Nashua, New Hampshire 03062
Tel: (603) 886-1743 • Fax: (603) 595-9010

Cay Gregg assisted in the research.
Cover design by Bedford Granite Group
Printed by Puritan Press, Inc., Hollis, New Hampshire

Printed in the United States of America

Amos Tuck (1810-1870)

Special Acknowledgments

The writers are deeply grateful for the research, advice and guidance given in the preparation of this document by the following historians:

Nancy C. Merrill, Director of Collections, Exeter Historical Society

James L. Garvin, New Hampshire State Architectural Historian

William M. Gardner, New Hampshire Secretary of State

Frank C. Mevers, New Hampshire State Archivist

CONTENTS

THE FIRST "REPUBLICAN" PARTY

The name "Republican" as applied to a political party was first used in 1801 when Thomas Jefferson was elected President of the United States as a Democratic-Republican. He was succeeded by James Madison, James Monroe, and John Quincy Adams, all of whom won on the Democratic-Republican ticket.

In June of 1828, when John Quincy Adams was running for re-election against Andrew Jackson, "The Friends Of The Administration" held a convention in Concord, New Hampshire, to choose electors for "The National Republican Ticket." But Jackson won, became the first Democratic President, and thus established the Democratic Party.

Yet the first national "Republican" convention was not called until 1831 when Henry Clay was nominated for president. Prior to that time candidates for president and vice president had been selected by Congressional caucus, or other methods, without national political conventions. After Clay's defeat no "Republican" conventions were held until 1856. Meanwhile, most of the former "Republicans" became Whigs.

New Hampshire Congressman Ichabod Bartlett, keynote speaker at the Concord convention in 1828, became a delegate to the 1831 convention held in Baltimore. William H. Y. Hackett of Portsmouth was one of the secretaries in the 1828 convention, and New Hampshire Congressman William Plumer, Jr., played an influential role in the proceedings. It is important to remember the names of these leaders of the first "Republican" party because they became close associates of Amos Tuck. All three later attended the first "Republican" meeting in Exeter of October 12, 1853.

The National Republican Ticket

E Pluribus Unum

For President
John Quincy Adams

For Vice President
Richard Rush

For Electors
George Sullivan, of Exeter
Samuel Quarles, of Ossipee
Samuel Sparhawk, of Concord
William Bixby, of Francestown
Nahum Parker, of Portsmouth
Thomas Woolson, of Claremont
Ezra Bartlett, of Haverhill
Ephraim H. Mahurin, of Columbia

Assembled at the Capitol in
Concord, June 12, 1828

THE REPUBLICAN PARTY OF LINCOLN

The party we now refer to as "Republican" elected Abraham Lincoln as its president in 1860. At its first convention in 1856, John Fremont, the nominee, had been an unsuccessful candidate.

It is this party which Amos Tuck named in Exeter on October 12, 1853.

WHO WAS AMOS TUCK?

Born in Parsonsfield, Maine, August 2, 1810, Amos was the second son and fourth child of John and Betsey (Towle) Tuck. His father, John, had moved from Hampton, New Hampshire, where six generations of the family had lived, because he inherited a small farm of moderate size in that thinly settled region of Maine. Amos remained there only seventeen years, when he set off on his own to enter the academy of Effingham, New Hampshire, where he began preparing for college while teaching during the winters.

He taught at Pembroke Academy, and was later employed as preceptor at Hampton Academy while studying law. He graduated from Dartmouth College in 1835. Admitted to the New Hampshire bar in November of 1838, he soon became the partner of Hon. James Bell of Exeter, who subsequently became a U.S. Senator.

Amos' older sibling, Jonathan, served as Mayor of Biddeford, Maine, for eighteen years. His younger brother, John, was an agricultural expert, author, and friend of Jeremiah W. Dearborn, an author whose biography of Amos Tuck was published in 1904.

Amos was twice married and had eight children, only three of whom survived to adulthood. His son, Edward, became the most famous, both here and abroad. He was the benefactor of Dartmouth College who established the Amos Tuck School of Business Administration and whose generous support made possible the construction of the New Hampshire Historical Society building at 30 Park Street in Concord.

"A colleague in that Congress (1847–1853) with whom Mr. Tuck formed a strong friendship was a plain, awkward man from Illinois—Abraham Lincoln."

—Genealogical & Family History of the State of N.H.

TUCK ENTERS POLITICS, FORMS THE INDEPENDENT DEMOCRATS

1842: Amos Tuck was elected to the New Hampshire House of Representatives as a Democrat.

1844: Then-Chairman of the Democratic Central Committee Franklin Pierce deprived Amos Tuck's close colleague, John P. Hale, of re-nomination to Congress because of Hale's opposition to slavery and to the annexation of Texas. Never before had a national issue so affected state politics. Pierce had traveled all over New Hampshire to solicit support against Hale, encountering little opposition until he met John L. Hayes of Portsmouth and Amos Tuck of Exeter. David A. Gregg, Henry F. French, and N. Porter Cram were three additional prominent Democrats who also stood up for Hale.

Dissatisfied with Democratic party principles and its position favorable to slavery, Tuck made the decision that was to alter dramatically the course of his political life. He broke with the Democratic leaders on the question of slavery and the admission of Texas, and was formally cast out of the Democratic party in 1844. "The state has been cursed with dictation of small men for years," Tuck told Hale, "and I am willing for a division; if that becomes inevitable in consequence of your doing your duty." (*Exeter News-Letter*).

On January 7, 1845, Congressman John P. Hale wrote his now famous letter to his constituents whom he addressed as "Democratic-Republican electors," explaining his refusal to vote for the annexation of Texas and its resultant expansion of slavery, which he felt was being done in an unconstitutional manner. "If you shall think differently from me on this subject, and

should therefore deem it expedient to select another person to effectuate your purpose in Congress, no person in the state will bow more submissively to your will than myself."

"While it is true that Mr. Hale did not take part in our early movements, except in the letter which first roused them," explained John Lord Hayes, Hale's "unusual address of the letter to Democratic-Republican Electors is remarkable as a prediction of the future of the Republican party."

Tuck began a movement that would decimate the control which the Democratic party had exerted in New Hampshire politics for over a decade. In Tuck's large collection of letters to friends and colleagues, he often referred to the "secret" enterprises and alliances he was painstakingly cultivating in favor of his cause. "His separation from his original party was as creditable to his sense of right as to his political sagacity," wrote Charles H. Bell in 1889.

February 22, 1845: Amos Tuck called a convention to form an independent movement in support of John P. Hale. He succeeded in securing 263 signatures for this petition. The Convention was held in the vestry of the First Church in Exeter, where the first crystallized opposition to the extension of slavery was formed. "It was the first successful rebellion, anywhere in the country," said Amos Tuck, in his introduction to the *Exeter News-Letter* series he began on February 18, 1876.

"No one who reads the call can fail to see that it embodies all that is distinctive of the Free Soil, and its successor, the Republican party," wrote John Lord Hayes. Shown on the next page is a copy of a heliotype plate of the call from a photograph of the only copy then extant, a broadside of about 18 x 12 inches, the emblematical frame having been carved by hand.

6

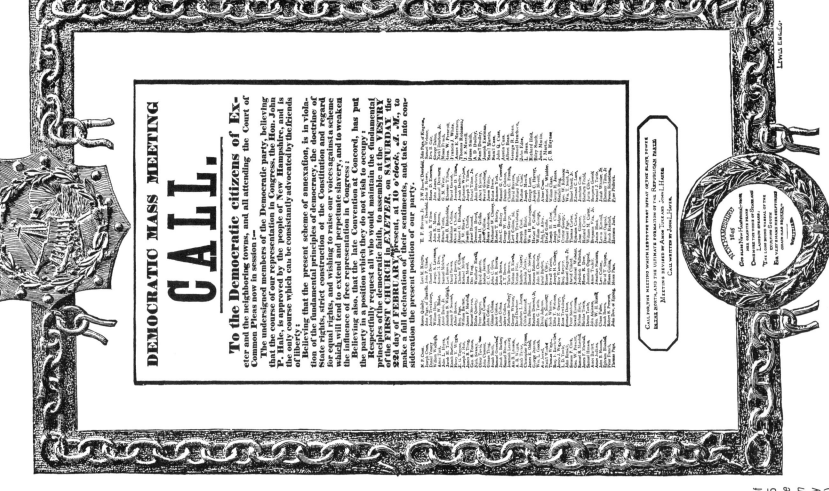

Call to the Meeting of
February 22, 1845
(*A Reminiscence of the
Free-Soil Movement in
New Hampshire* by
John L. Hayes, 1885)

John L. Hayes, in his letter to the *Exeter News-Letter*, November 25, 1879, remembered that after Franklin Pierce had publicly resolved to "throw Hale overboard," to which Hayes had strongly protested, he received a letter from Amos Tuck which stated unequivocally to Pierce that if Mr. Hale was to be expelled from the party on account of his opposition to slavery, he was himself ready to be expelled likewise. John L. Hayes had been the only other man who had so expressed himself to Pierce. The letter led to a mutual understanding and close fellowship between Tuck and Hayes. Along with N.P. Cram and his brother, Joseph, "they visited several towns, worked themselves and set others to work, and soon the papers came back with two hundred and sixty-three names, in all, attached."

The letter continued:

> The call for the meeting was then printed as a handbill, with all the names attached, and stuck up throughout the country. At the time appointed, the 22nd of February, the roads were nearly impassable; yet a meeting was held, respectable in numbers and unparalleled in spirit, in which speeches were made by Professor J. G. Hoyt of Exeter, John Dow of Epping, Austin Cass of Candia, by Mr. Tuck, myself, and others, and organization effected. An address to the people of New Hampshire, and resolutions, were adopted, and after the meeting extensively circulated, as far as they could be without a press at our service. [A copy of those resolutions is on record.]

"Without doubt the Exeter convention became the nucleus of the Republican party."

Genealogical & Family History of the State of New Hampshire

Amos Tuck's own series for the *Exeter News-Letter* in 1876 recounts in minute detail the organizational effort of 1845. A brief excerpt from Article VII, reads as follows:

> When the day of the meeting arrived, leading Democrats collected at the Squamscot House (also known as Blake's Hotel) directly opposite the place of meeting, and watched with great interest the signs of success or failure of the advertised gathering. A great thaw in the accumulated snows of the winter had just taken place, the weather was still warm, and the roads in many places were nearly impassable. The writer of this sketch had likewise gone to the Squamscot House, to watch for the earliest arrival, ready to join the first man that should appear on the steps of the vestry. A half hour and more after the time of meeting had passed and no one appeared. The Democratic leaders pronounced the whole thing a failure, and lavished their efforts at wit, to make it ridiculous. Provoked and mortified, yet resolute to go forward under any circumstances, the writer went alone to the steps of the vestry and sat down facing the collection opposite, who were loudly exultant over the supposed abortion of the meeting. Soon John Dow of Epping, N.P. Cram of Hampton Falls, John L. Hayes of Portsmouth, Austin Cass of Candia, and others, gathered around the vestry door, with good cheer and courage in their countenances, when the Democratic spectators speedily separated, each going to his own place. The meeting was soon organized, with N.P. Cram, President, Abraham Emerson of Candia, Secretary, and a Committee to report resolutions and an address for publication. The meeting was addressed in a succession of spirited speeches by the persons above mentioned, and by others, forenoon and afternoon, the utmost enthusiasm prevailed, and the numbers who attended exceeded the combined numbers of both the Whig and Democratic Conventions, which had been held in the same place a few days before. This meeting consolidated the organization of the Independent Democracy. It was the first meeting of the protestants against party which

assembled in the State, after the official decapitation of Mr. Hale. Such sentiments were avowed, and such action taken, as committed the 261 men who had called the meeting, and all who had attended it, to irreconcilable opposition to the action of their former party. An address and resolutions, carefully prepared in advance, by the writer of this sketch and Prof. J. G. Hoyt, were adopted, and subsequently circulated as extensively as possible throughout the State. The movement at Exeter became generally known, and extensively approved, and meetings of a similar character were held in sundry other towns, where resolutions were adopted approving the action at Exeter, and promising persistent maintenance of the principles set forth.

———◆◆———

An organization was then and there effected, which gathered power, through personal and printed appeals to the people, to make itself formidable enough, by the election in March, to defeat Mr. Hale's opponent; and ultimately, with the Legislature itself, not only to replace Mr. Hale in Congress, but to raise him to the United States Senate for the long term.

George E. Street, January 11, 1880.

———◆◆———

Hale and Tuck formed a new party consisting of a coalition of abolitionists who called themselves "Independent Democrats." With the help of George G. Fogg, Tuck promptly established a newspaper of that name, first published on May 1, 1845, in Manchester, and later in Concord. Said Tuck, "It became impor-

tant to have an organ, through which we could have access to the public ear. Our opposition to our party had become a power, more or less influential in every part of the state." Tuck and Joseph G. Hoyt, Professor of Greek and Mathematics at Exeter Academy, wrote most of the editorials during 1845.

In February of 1845, Hayes published an elaborately prepared speech in Hale's defense.

> **This was the first printed speech or protest in the movement which revolutionized the State, with the exception of the letter of Mr. Hale; and I may be permitted to say that Henry Wilson expressed to me, personally, his regret that he had not mentioned this circumstance in his work, *The Rise and Fall of the Slave Power in America*. Mr. Tuck, in reply to an attack of the *Patriot*, had published a letter of defense.**

Hayes explains further that the election came, and Democratic candidate John Woodbury was defeated by John P. Hale:

> **This was the first chapter in the work of emancipating New Hampshire from proslavery Democracy, and the most important chapter,—the first, I believe in the great work of making antislavery views triumphant in political action throughout the country...the beginning was in New Hampshire, when the backbone of Democracy was wrenched, if not broken, in 1845. [Editor's Note: The word "Democracy" refers to the Democratic Party.]**

Mr. Hayes describes convincingly the influence of the *Independent Democrat* and how the movement in New Hampshire had an immediate influence upon adjoining States.

He concludes emphatically:

> After the defeat of Mr. Woodbury, and the determination to elect Mr. Hale to the Senate, some of my friends in the movement sug-

gested to me that my name should be used as a candidate for Congress. I unhesitatingly declined, declaring that this honor belonged pre-eminently to Mr. Tuck, not only for his services and talents, but his organizing power; and events have proved that, next to defending Mr. Hale, I rendered the best service to the cause in supporting your distinguished fellow-townsman.

The *Independent Democrat* "advocated Republicanism for eleven years before the Republican party came into being," Tuck would write later.

The paper carried reports of speeches by Hale at meetings in Dover, Exeter, and Manchester, all well-attended. The energy and determination of the Independents in launching so vigorous a campaign were indomitable. The "Hale Democracy" was becoming a formidable force. The Independent-Democrats claimed consistently, as the February 22nd convention in Exeter had resolved, that a direct or indirect advocacy of slavery, or support of those measures which will foster and encourage it, was wholly inconsistent with the doctrines of human equality and universal justice.

"At meetings throughout Rockingham County, the southern part of Carroll, and the eastern area of Merrimack, Hale, usually accompanied by Amos Tuck, hammered away at the themes of opposition to southern and party dictation," wrote Steven Paul McGiffen, Ph.D., *Prelude to Republicanism: Issues in the Realignment of Political Parties in New Hampshire, 1835–1847* (1984). The two men's speeches had a profound influence on the growing movement which climaxed in a Fourth of July rally of 2,000 people in Moultonborough during the summer of 1845. "The gathering was an important symbol that the new party could rival the Democrats for organisational (sic) skill

and vitality, that it was not a mere passing protest and that its support had grown rather than dwindled since March," added McGiffen.

Through the months following the Convention of 1845, Tuck never ceased nor relented, tenaciously expanding the base of his young party, one-by-one. In preparation for a mass meeting of Independents and Liberty men in Newmarket, in mid-September, 1846, Tuck wrote to George G. Fogg: "I hope everything is going well for our independent cause….I wish to say privately that George Barstow is nearly resolved to go with us."

In a letter to John L. Carlton, Esq., of Bath, NH, dated September 16, 1846, Tuck wrote:

> I embrace this opportunity to say that our Independent cause does not lag in this part of the State. It is onward and the people will support the good cause for future elections. We are coalescing with the Liberty men who stand with us in sentiment. You will see in the Independent Democrat and E. Freeman an account of our meeting at New Market, and certain resolutions offered by me at that meeting unanimously passed. I hope they will meet your approbation. They will show you the tendency of our sentiments. Let me hear from you at your leisure.

Tuck and his influential associates worked feverishly for that cause, which had taken on distinct "Republican" overtones. The Democratic party suffered severe fragmentation. Tuck's leadership would bring about a recognition which he had not sought nor anticipated: both he and John P. Hale were chosen to represent New Hampshire in Washington.

DEMOCRATIC MASS MEETING.

CALL.

To the Democratic citizens of Exeter and the neighboring towns, and all attending the Court of Common Pleas now in session:

The undersigned members of the Democratic party, believing that the course of our representative[1] in Congress, Hon. John P. Hale, is approved by the people of New Hampshire, and is the only course which can be consistently advocated by the friends of liberty;

Believing that the present scheme of (the) annexation (of Texas) is in violation of the fundamental principles of Democracy, the doctrine of States rights, strict construction of the Constitution, and regard for equal rights, and wishing to raise our voices against a scheme which will tend to extend and perpetuate slavery, and to weaken the influence of free representation in Congress;

Believing, also, that the late Convention at Concord has put the party in a position which they do not wish to occupy;

Respectfully request all who would maintain the fundamental principles of the Democratic faith to assemble at the vestry of the First Church in Exeter, on Saturday, the 22d day of February, present (1845), at 10 o'clock, A. M., to make a full declaration of their sentiments, and take into consideration the present position of our party.

N. P. Cram.
Joseph Cram.
Daniel Veasey.
William Wadleigh.
Amos Tuck.
John L. Hayes.
Jacob M. Towle.
Enoch Bartlett.
Henry Y. Wiggin.
E. G. Tappan.
Joseph J. Hoit.
James R. Thing.
Geo. S. Yeaton.
Nath. Swasey.
Oliver Towle, 3d.
John Clement.
Gilman Thing.

Albert Knowls.
Sewell Goodhue.
James Willey.
Rufus Drew.
Solomon York.
Samuel G. Carswell.
Dennis Colman.
Charles C. French.
David Stevens.
Hilliard Fogg.
Nathan Chase.

Josiah Smith.
Samuel Greenleaf.
Josiah G. Barker.
Samuel Hanson.
Jeremiah Leavitt.
Asa B. Lamson.
A. R. Wiggin.
Jacob Taylor.
Christopher Rymes.
James E. Odell.
George Janvrin.
Wm. L. Gooch.
Asa Jewell.
Nath'l Weeks.
Thomas Wiggin.
Benjamin P. Batchelder.
James J. Wiggin.

Wm. T. Smith, Jr.
Daniel Merrill, Jr.
Edmund C. Lane.
Jonathan Cass.
Sherburn Fifield.
Justin Cilley.
Benjamin Gerrish.
Samuel J. Tuttle.
Josiah Whittier, Jr.
Ebenezer Tilton. Jr.
Person Richardson.

L. D. Fowle.
John Remick.
Simeon P. Clark.
Geo. W. Prescott.
Samuel S. Marshall.
James F. Marshall.
Samuel Hanson.
Amos Bartlett.
Amos Judkins.
John B. Hanson.
Ephraim Blaisdell.
Peter Froude.
Thomas Page.
Aaron Quimby.
John Page, of Danville.
Josiah Tewksbury.
William Hoyt.

Thomas Robinson.
J. S. Morrill.
Jesse Smith.
A. D. Dudley.
Sam'l Dudley.
Joseph Eastman.
Sam'l Martin.
Sam'l Cass.
John Q. Cass.
Austin Cass.
Albert Bean.

Joseph W. Blake.
Amos Davis, Jr.
Jonathan S. Wadleigh.
Joseph P. Secomb.
Albert Brown.
Benj. Page.
William Bartlett.
James F. Marshall.
Samuel Stevens.
Elisha Quimby.
Peter Sargent.
Bernard Currier.
John Collins.
Gilman Collins.
Jacob Collins.
Laban Collins.
Jabez Collins.
Nathaniel Bradley.
George Whittier.
David Dearborn.
Jonathan L. James.
Calvin Eastman.
Oren Dimond.
Reuben Dimond.
John G. Tuttle.
David Johnson.
Benj. S. Sanborn.
Jacob Whittier.
Elihu T. Webster.
Jesse E. Gorge.
Enos Tewksbury.
Samuel Dunn.
Peter Sanborn.
Sewall Eastman.
Nathan Hoyt.
Hichlas Towle.
Darius Towle.
John Atkinson.
Geo. W. H. Morrill.
Chase Fuller.
Josiah Brown.
Robert S. Prescott.
John Dow, of Epping.
Levi M. Knight.
John P. Chase.
Daniel Dow.
Joseph S. Lawrence.
Samuel H. Dow.
Joseph Merrill.
George Lane.
Joseph C. Harvey.
Daniel Merrill.
Abner Cram.
Samuel L. Whidder.
William Chase.
George H. James.
Shediah Ring.
Geo. W. Robinson.

David Brown.
Sewel Brown.
Charles F. Chase.
Richard Morrill.
Jona. Morrill.
Otis Wing.
Woodbury Marsh.
David Janvrin.
Joshua Janvrin.
C. C. Gove.
John C. Gove.
John B. Brown.
Jacob Brown.
J. T. Brown.
Thos. Brown.
Nathan B. Marsh.
Nathan Pike.
Matthew Nealey.
Bowdin Nealey.
Daniel C. Sleeper.
Simeon Robinson.
John H. Chesley.
Israel Bartlett.
Moses Cilley.
Sewall Watson.
Joseph H. Chesley.
Rice Watson.
Benj. Sawyer.
Samuel Sargent, Jr.
David Clifford.
Nathaniel Webster.
Jedediah Philbrick.
Moses R. Dow.
Jonathan Osgood.
Amos Tucker.
Jonathan Sanborn.
Levi Collins.
David T. Sleeper.
Moses Collins.
Moses Page.
E. F. Stevens, Jr., of Deerfield.
Josiah R. Tilton.
John K. Moore.
John H. Brown.
Stoten Tuttle.
John B. Batchelder.
Jonathan Collins.
Oren M. Challis.
Peter Philbrick.
John Page, of Kingston.
Samuel Webster.
Ezra B. Gale.
George Dalton.
Nath'l Dearborn, Jr.
Moses French.
Geo. W. Prescott.
Francis J. White.
Amos E. Morrison.

Joseph Challis.
Israel Dimond.
Jeremiah Beard.
John H. Griffin.
Jacob Collins.
Moses Anderson.
Nathaniel W. Cheney.
Robert T. Shirley.
John C. Bradley.
George W. Buswell.
Lyman George.
Levi Collins, 2d.
Amos Tewksbury.
Joseph Cook.
Stevens Blake.
Wm. H. Huntington.
Harlan P. Griffin.
William George.
John L. Allen.
David Griffin.
Joseph H. Allen.
Joseph H. Challis.
William Badger.
Currier George.
Daniel Page.
Thomas Carter.
Ephraim Carter.
Jesse Gilmore.
Richard Carter.
William M. Carter.
Benjamin Fitz, Jr.
James Hook.
Lewis Kimball.
Daniel Osgood.
Jacob Randall.
Harrison Jack.
John S. Rowe.
J. W. James, of Deerfield.
Moses D. Emerson.
John James.
Samuel Dearborn.
G. M. Wear.
Ebenezer Tilton.
David Gerrish.
Jeremiah D. Tilton.
Josiah Dudley.
Ephraim Winslow.
Joseph T. Tilton.

George R. Bean.
Samuel Dearborn.
John Edes.
L. Bean.
Richard Hoit.
Biley Smith.
Jona. Martin.
J. Martin.
C. B. Haynes.

List of attendees at meeting of February 22, 1845

Congregational Church in Exeter

Exeter Historical Society

Located at 21 Front Street, directly opposite Gorham Hall (Blake's Hotel), the original building was begun in 1798. Radically altered in 1838, it is still used today as a place of worship and center of community activity. In its vestry, on February 22, 1845, Amos Tuck and John L. Hayes wrote the resolutions which were enacted on the same day by the convention of Democrats called by Amos Tuck. The action of this assembly resulted in the endorsement of John P. Hale as a candidate for the United States Senate, and the founding of the new and separate "Independent Democrats."

JOHN P. HALE AND AMOS TUCK ELECTED TO CONGRESS

The Independent movement, which seemed so hopeless at first, resulted in the election of John P. Hale to the U.S. Senate in 1846, and of Mr. Tuck to Congress in 1847.

—*Genealogical & Family History of the State of N.H.*

Referring to his own election to the Congress in 1847, Tuck clearly stated:

From this period dates the Republican organization in the Granite State, though the name Republican was not adopted until the Convention at Philadelphia, which nominated Fremont and Dayton in 1856. The success in New Hampshire influenced the whole country.
—*From Amos Tuck's own handwritten autobiography*

Political events, in both state and nation, had driven Whigs, abolitionists, and some Democrats together in a coalition which, if it were based on expediency, had also a basis in mutually-held beliefs. This, then, was New Hampshire's 'prelude' to the Republicanism of the 1850s.

—*Steven Paul McGiffen*

Abraham Lincoln of Illinois was also elected a new member of the 30th United States Congress. Tuck and Lincoln became close friends, a relationship which brought Lincoln's son, Robert, as a student to Phillips Exeter Academy in 1859. Amos would be recompensed for his loyalty and friendship, when Lincoln became President.

John P. Hale stood out as an influential United States Senator from the beginning. Wrote Richard H. Sewell in *John P. Hale and the Politics of Abolition,*

It was well that Hale possessed such popularity, for his role in the Senate was a difficult one. **For two years he stood virtually alone in that body as spokesman for the antislavery movement.... It meant that his words attracted the special attention of all political groups, and it gave him the moral support of antislavery men from all parts of the United States—not just New Hampshire.**

Wrote Charles Sumner to John Greenleaf Whittier: "Thank God! At last we have a voice in the Senate. Hale has opened well."

THE LITERATI WERE WITH THE REPUBLICANS

The literati were with the Republicans:
Whittier wrote its campaign songs
Lowell translated its doctrines into poetry
Emerson, Bryant, Longfellow, Holmes
and Motley were all members."

—Wilfred E. Binkley

The poet Whittier, between whom and Mr. Tuck existed an intimate sympathy and friendship, broke forth into a paean of joy when New Hampshire, until then the strongest Democratic state in the north, escaped from party control and placed in the senate of the United States its first Anti-Slavery member, John P. Hale.

The poem, 'New Hampshire, 1845,' begins:

God bless New Hampshire! From her granite peaks
Once more the voice of Stark and Langdon speaks.
The long-bound vassal of the exulting South
For very shame her self-forged chain has broken;
Torn the black seal of slavery from her mouth,
And in the clear tones of her old time spoken!
Oh, all undreamed-of, all uphoped-for changes!
The Tyrant's ally proves his sternest foe;
To all his biddings, from her mountain ranges,
New Hampshire thunders an indignant No!

—Genealogical & Family History of the State of N.H.

John Greenleaf Whittier is often referred to as antislavery's poet laureate. Richard H. Sewell wrote:

Ever since the day in 1835 when he and George Thompson had had to flee before a hostile mob in Concord, New Hampshire, Whittier had taken a special interest in the "redemption" of that state. Hale's bold stand on Texas delighted him, and he was among the first to congratulate the New Hampshire representative for his letter to his constituents: "I would rather be the author of that

John Greenleaf Whittier, anti-slavery's
poet laureate and friend of Amos Tuck

letter than the President of the United States. Under all circumstances, it is one of the boldest and noblest words ever spoken for Liberty." And among the abolitionists of New Hampshire and Massachusetts he drummed up support for Hale.

Another of Whittier's poems, 'A Letter,' refers to the contest in New Hampshire, which resulted in the defeat of the pro-slavery Democracy and Hale's election. It is crammed full of local allusions and names messrs. Tuck, Hale and Hayes.

There Hayes and Tuck as nurses sat,
As near as near could be, man;
They leeched him with the "Democrat;"
They blistered with the Freeman.

—Boston Chronotype 1846

TUCK RETURNS TO EXETER

1853: Having served three consecutive terms in Washington, Tuck, too, had become a national figure, while still in his thirties. The state's Democrats had vowed to get even and concentrated their efforts to unseat him. Thus, he failed to be re-elected for a fourth term, and returned to Exeter. Hale served one six-year term, and ran against Franklin Pierce for President of the United States on the Free Soil Ticket in 1852. Hale would serve again in the Senate from 1855-65 and became a Republican.

Upon his return to Exeter, Tuck started at once a movement to unite all minor political factions in the state into a new coalition. During the summer of 1853 he contacted leaders of the Whigs, Free Soilers, Independent Democrats and former Democrats who had been purged from the party...

—William H. Mandrey

From the *Dictionary of American Biography,* 1936:

Defeated for a fourth term because of a temporary waning of anti-slavery fervor in his state together with an effective gerrymander by the legislature (1853), Tuck continued active in the movement against slavery, but his essential sanity and political acumen kept him out of its more extravagant manifestations and his activity was therefore vastly more effective—so effective, indeed, that his admirers have often claimed that the Republican party was really a New Hampshire creation. At all events, he was instrumental in 1853 and 1854 in bringing about a merger of the dissatisfied into a new party alignment.

Feb. 3, 1853: Horace Greeley, a New Hampshire native, Tuck colleague in Congress, and founder of the New York Tribune, gave a speech at the Lyceum in Exeter about Henry Clay, founder of the Whig party, in which he said: "He (Clay) was an ardent Republican, in times when Republicanism was the right arm of the country, and as such, he was chosen to fill various places requiring the confidence of the people, not only in the Kentucky legislature, but in the U.S. Senate and House." —*Exeter News-Letter*, Feb. 7, 1853 (Mr. Tuck had maintained a close relationship with Greeley. Tuck was very active in the Lyceum and had served as its Chairman, though it is not known whether he attended that particular meeting in February.)

Tuck called several public meetings throughout New Hampshire during that spring and summer, expanding his movement. On August 31, 1853, he presided at a meeting of The Friends of Freedom, in Wolfeboro, attended by over two thousand. Slavery in general and the Fugitive Slave Law were discussed. John P. Hale was saluted and it was resolved that similar local meetings should be held throughout the state.

Oct. 3, 1853 Editorial in *Exeter News-Letter:*

> In our own state—the Gibraltar of the dominant party—no one can be ignorant that there is at work a mighty undercurrent which is fast sweeping the Democracy from their chosen moorings. While our renegade Whigs begin to see that they have rolled their best coat in the mud for nought, the unterrified have scented the baneful idea that politicians, like patriots, sometimes fail of their reward in this life. In truth, we believe New Hampshire never exhibited such an array of sorry Democratic faces as at present.

TUCK CALLS HISTORIC MEETING AT BLAKE'S HOTEL

October 12, 1853: Tuck called a meeting of Anti-Slavery men of all parties with a view to better co-operation and united action. The meeting was held, October 12, 1853, at Major Blake's hotel, later the Squamscott House, in Exeter, and on this occasion Mr. Tuck proposed the name Republican for the new party. The credit for the christening is usually given to Horace Greeley; but his suggestion was not made till the next year; and the great honor of the name belongs to Amos Tuck.

from *Genealogical and Family History of the State of N.H.*, and supported by many other historians in subsequent biographies of Tuck.

Fourteen prestigious leaders joined together at Blake's Hotel, October 12, 1853.

Hobart Pillsbury, *New Hampshire, A History,* Lewis Historical Publishing Co., N.Y. 1927:

> There were four political parties opposed to the Democratic party and in 1853 a convention was held at Exeter to consolidate these factions. At this convention Amos Tuck proposed that all four of the parties drop their present names and adopt the name Republican, to which everybody agreed. This was the first time that the Republican name was ever used in the United States as belonging to what is now the present Republican party.

William H. Mandrey, "How the Republicans Got Their Name," *N.H. Echoes*, July–Aug. 1972:

> **There can be no doubt that the plan to form a new party originated in Exeter, that Amos Tuck gave the party its name, and that Horace Greeley gave the name to the nation.**

Amos Tuck's Law Office

ATTENDEES AT MEETING OF OCTOBER 12, 1853

Amos Tuck of Exeter, Dartmouth College. Lawyer. Three-term U.S. Congressman 1847–53; considered for Cabinet position by Abraham Lincoln in 1860. Trustee of Dartmouth College, Phillips Exeter Academy, and Robinson Female Seminary.

John Parker Hale of Rochester, Bowdoin College. Free Soiler, Independent Democrat; NH Legislature 1832–34; U.S. Congressman 1843–45; first anti-slavery United States Senator, 1847–53, 1855–65 (ran as Republican in 1858); U.S. presidential nominee on Liberty Party, 1847, and Free Soil ticket, 1852; U.S. minister to Spain, 1865–69.

Ichabod Bartlett of Portsmouth, Whig, Dartmouth College graduate, NH Speaker of the House, 1821–22. U.S. Congressman, 1823–29. Founder of N.H. Historical Society. "Dartmouth college case." From 1828 speech: "His (Andrew Jackson) public conduct has been at war with all our Republican feelings and principles." [Bartlett died shortly after the October meeting. "Recently the grave has closed over Ichabod Bartlett, one of the most accomplished lawyers and orators of our native State." —Henry Wilson's speech, Boston, November 2, 1853.]

Asa McFarland of Concord, Whig leader. Book and job printer, business established June 1850; bought the New Hampshire Statesman with partner, Edwin Jenks, which was published until October 1, 1871, then went into possession of the Republican Press Association. [Jenks later became Secretary of the N.H. Republican State Committee, 1877–78.]

George G. Fogg of Gilmanton. Dartmouth; Harvard Law School. Founder, Independent Democrat. NH Secretary of State, 1846–47. Member, NH House of Representatives. U.S. Senator (serving out unexpired term) 1866–67. Member of first Republican National Committee, elected temporary Secretary of its first National Convention in 1856. Attended the Convention's planning meeting in Pittsburg, February 22, 1856. Appointed by President Lincoln as Minister for the U.S. to Switzerland.

William Plumer, Jr., of Epping. Phillips Exeter Academy and Harvard. NH House of Representatives and NH Senate. U.S. Congressman, 1819–1825. Son of William, a Senator and NH Governor.

William H. Y. Hackett of Portsmouth. Dartmouth College. Lawyer, journalist with the Portsmouth Journal for fifty years; bank president; served in N.H.House of Representatives 1851-52-57-60-67-68-69; NH Senator 1861–63, President of NH State Senate 1862–63. President of NH Historical Society. President of 1864 electors.

Dr. Daniel Homer Batchelder of Londonderry. Practiced medicine in Londonderry for several years. Medical education from Norwich University, Vermont, and Berkshire Medical College, Pittsfield, Mass. Member of N.H., Mass., and Rhode Island medical societies. A surgeon, he served in Burnsides Corps during the Civil War. Was U.S. Counsel to Londonderry, Ireland.

John Preston of New Ipswich. Harvard College, 1823. Lawyer. Free Soiler; N.H., House of Representatives 1833, 1838, 1843–1853; only State Senator who was not a Democrat, 1848–50; Free Soil candidate for Congress in 1848 and 1852. He and Fogg were delegates to the Free Soil Convention of August 9, 1848 in Buffalo, New York, and of August 11, 1852, in Pittsburgh, PA. Republican delegate in 1856.

Major Abraham Blake of Exeter. Proprietor of Blake's Hotel.

William Wadleigh of Exeter, son of town selectman; NH House of Representatives 1846-1848; law partner of Francis O. French for 2–3 years. "Mr. Wadleigh long enjoyed the confidence of his townsmen and was repeatedly called by them to assist in the management of municipal affairs."—*Exeter News-Letter* death notice, July 1867.

David Currier of Auburn, prominent Whig, candidate for "Counsellor" and a supporter of Tuck in 1847 election; cashier of the Derry State Bank from 1856–75; moderator; selectman of Chester, 1829–30; NH House of Representatives 1832–33, 1836–37, 1840; selectman of Auburn, 1847; deacon of Central Cong. Church, Derry.

John Young of Portsmouth, Member of committee to draft resolutions for Whig Convention in June 1847 which supported Tuck in his election to the Congress.

John B. Wentworth of Salmon Falls.

> In particular, these fourteen men were shocked at the popular sovereignty notion of Stephen A. Douglas, Democratic Senator from Illinois, which had been embodied in the Kansas-Nebraska Act of that same year. The *Exeter News-Letter* is full of accounts of atrocities done to slaves as Southerners rushed into Kansas to convert it to a slave state.
>
> Thomas C. Hayden in a Phillips Exeter Academy
article on "Abraham Lincoln and the Formation
of the Republican Party in New Hampshire."

Dr. J. Duane Squires, noted State Historian, recounted the circumstances of the October 12th meeting in The Granite State of the United States, 1956:

> In February, 1853, at the close of his third two-year term in the House, Congressman Tuck delivered a strong speech, stressing what later would have been called Republican sentiments, and came home to continue his opposition to the extension of slavery. His idea was to unify all the elements in New Hampshire which had any reason to oppose the Democrats, and from them to make a new and militant party. Ready to hand were such splinter groups as the old Independent Democrats of 1845; the remains of the Free Soil and Liberty parties in the State; the Whigs, now in a declining condition both on the State and national levels; the temperance advocates; and the "Know-Nothing" party which was temporarily strong in New Hampshire during the early 1850s. On October 12, 1853, Tuck met with thirteen other men in Blake's Hotel in Exeter. Among the influential politicians present were John P. Hale, then out of the Senate; George G. Fogg, the newspaper editor from Concord; Asa McFarland, a Whig leader from the capital city; Ichabod Bartlett, a Whig chieftain from Portsmouth; Dr. D.H. Batchelder from Londonderry; and William Plumer, a son of the famous political figure of a half century before. Seeking to form an organization that would work harmoniously together, Tuck suggested that they abandon all old names and call themselves Republicans.
>
> These deliberations were, of course, secret, and no newspaper accounts appeared at the time to tell what had happened at Exeter….

Noted State Historian **Elwin L. Page**, *Abraham Lincoln in New Hampshire,* Houghton-Miflin, 1929, recounting the meeting of October 12, 1853, and Tuck's suggestion that the four factions unite under the name Republican as unanimously approved: **"Thus was projected the first Republican party in any state."**

December 1853: The meeting of October 12th had been kept secret. No record was kept—perhaps, theoretically, because some of its attendees were running for public office under different party banners. But Tuck's colleague, Horace Greeley had visited Exeter in early February, returning in December for his annual Christmas visit. Born in Amherst, Greeley had lived in Londonderry where Daniel Homer Batchelder had been one of his boyhood friends.

In retrospect, it seems appropriate to their close relationship that upon meeting Greeley once again, Dr. Batchelder told him in confidence about the meeting of October 12th in Exeter, requesting Greeley not to print the new party name, "Republican," in his newspaper, the *New York Tribune*. Greeley had replied, "I think 'Republican' would be the best name, it will sound both Jeffersonian and Madisonian, and for that reason will take well."—from Batchelder's letter to the *Exeter News-Letter* of August 19, 1887.

Everett S. Stackpole, in his *History of New Hampshire,* Volume III, American Historical Society, N.Y., 1916, stated clearly:

> **The origin of the Republican party, then, may be traced back to the Exeter meeting of October 1853...Mr. Batchelder related the affair to Horace Greeley, while the latter was on vacation in his native town of Amherst.**

TUCK CONTINUES HOLDING STATEWIDE MEETINGS

December 12, 1853: The *Exeter News-Letter* reported a major "Free Soil" convention in Exeter comprised of a Senatorial Convention, the Rockingham County Convention, and a Rockingham Councilor Convention, followed by a mass meeting in which their uncompromising hostility to slavery was reiterated in the form of resolutions, the passage of which the Hon. Amos Tuck advocated in a stirring address to the assembly.

Feb. 14, 1854: Opponents of the Nebraska outrage held a meeting in Manchester City Hall. With a huge crowd in attendance, the Hon. William Plumer, former Congressman and one of the attendees at the October 1853 meeting, addressed the crowd "with powerful effect." "New Hampshire Moving—No Extension of Slavery" headed the record published in "Correspondence of the *N.Y. Tribune*" the following day, which continued, **"There is to be another meeting at Concord this evening, and soon another at Nashua, so, you see, New Hampshire is beginning to awake from her slumber of ages, and shake off the cobwebs of old parties."**

This reference to New Hampshire becomes important in its Republican history, proving that the Tuck movement had gained national attention very shortly after the meeting of October 12th.

Feb. 15, 1854: A public "Indignation Meeting" was called by James Bell, Tuck's law partner and a future U.S. Senator. "At a large and enthusiastic meeting of the citizens of Exeter, called, without distinction of party, to oppose the contemplated outrage upon the North, commonly known as the Nebraska bill, James Bell was elected chairman, F.B. Sanborn, Secretary, and Tuck gave a very strong speech and established resolutions against slavery." —*Exeter News-Letter*, Feb. 20, 1854

A LETTER FROM AMOS TUCK TO WILLIAM PLUMER, JR.

Exeter, Feb.14, 1854

Dear Sir:

An Anti-Nebraska meeting has been called at Exeter, tomorrow—Wednesday evening—hastily got up, and without concert. Can't you come and show yourself among us & say something. We should have announced your name among the speakers in a hand bill we have put up, had we felt authorised to do so. But we will make a place for you, if you will come, and shall feel obliged.

Resp. & truly yours,

Amos Tuck

Exeter Feb. 14, 1854 –

Dear Sir:

An Anti Nebraska meeting
has been called at Exeter, tomorrow
Wednesday evening – hastily got up,
and without Concert. Can't you come
and show yourself among us, & say some
thing – We should have announced your
name, in a hand bill we have put up, had
we felt authorized to to do. But we will
make a place for you, if you will come,
and shall feel obliged: –

 as among the Speakers

        Resp. & truly yours

        Amos Tuck

Hon Wm. Plumer –

Copy of Amos Tuck's handwritten letter to Wm. Plumer, Jr.
NH Historical Society

February 23, 1854: The same type of public meeting was held in Concord, and later in Manchester, the North Country, and Nashua. An invitation to William Plumer, Jr., from Asa McFarland and four other signees, demonstrates again that the group was enlarging throughout the state, recruiting new party members, as was Amos Tuck's stated objective. In August, 1854, a second large meeting was held in Wolfeboro, again led by Tuck and Hale.

March 8, 1854: William Plumer, Jr., spoke for an hour and ten minutes at an anti-Nebraska meeting, followed on March 13th by an hour-long address at Great Falls (near Dover) in response to an invitation from the Whig party.

Said Thomas R. Bright, "The Emergence of the Republican Party in New Hampshire, 1853–1857," *Historical New Hampshire*, Summer 1972:

> **There was no appreciable distinction between the Republican of 1857 and the Free Soil and Whig coalition of 1853....The 1856 national campaign provided an image and a name for a coalition already many years old.**

Oct. 2, 1854: Editorial in *Exeter News-Letter*:

> The old Anti-Slavery party now has as many aliases as Truth, or even as any rogue in Newgate. Its 'ups and downs' we have no heart to chronicle. Certainly its 'downs' have been numerous enough, and low enough; but its 'ups' are now in the ascendancy, and in some cases, it refuses very advantageous offers of matrimony from those who have regarded it, henceforth, as of humble origin, and doubtful destiny. **Today, the party is called 'Republican.' We remember when the little seed of this party, was planted in the torrid soil of this town.**

REPUBLICAN PARTY BORN IN EXETER

To the Editor of The Herald:

Last Saturday one of our local morning papers stated that the new "Progressive" party would be born at Jackson, Mich., "the historic spot where the Republican party was organized more than half a century ago." I strongly object to this statement, as there is very good evidence to show that the Republican party had its birth in Exeter, N. H., Oct. 12, 1853, at Maj. Blake's hotel, now known as the Squamscott Hotel. The name "Republican" was chosen and applied by the Hon. Amos Tuck, father of Mr. Edward Tuck of Paris, who recently gave New Hampshire its new historical building and who also gave $1,500,000 to Dartmouth College. Late in September, 1853, the Hon. Amos Tuck wrote this letter to Dr. Batchelder of Londonderry, N. H.:

Dear Sir: We deem it advisable to hold an informal meeting, composed of some of the principal members of the parties of this place (Exeter), on the 12th of October, at Maj. Blake's hotel. One of the principal objects of this informal meeting is to fix on a plan of harmonizing the different party organizations, whereby a more united cooperation can be secured, and the four parties may pull together under one title of organization. Hale, McFarland and Fogg will be present.

Yours respectfully.
AMOS TUCK.

The meeting was held and Congressman Tuck suggested that the comprehensive name "Republican" be given to the elements that were to constitute the new party.
HARRY V. LAWRENCE.
27 St. Stephen street. July 8.

Letter from
Harry V. Lawrence
to Boston Herald
Library of Congress

Gorham Hall. This large brick building at 24 Front Street called Gorham Hall, across the street from the Congregational Church, was built in 1851 as a hotel called the Squamscot House (Blake's Hotel). Here in 1853 Amos Tuck convened a meeting of abolitionist politicians from several political parties to discuss forming a new antislavery party. Since 1929 the site has been proclaimed as the location where the Republican Party was founded. The building has served as a hotel, a Phillips Exeter academy dormitory, and now an office building. It is a site designated in Exeter's "Historic Walk," along with all of Front Street. In July of 1995, the building was re-named "Major Blake's Hotel," in recognition of it's historical significance, by its owner, G. Albert "Bert" Bourgeois.

THE TUCK AND LINCOLN FRIENDSHIP EXTENDS TO EXETER

1856: Abraham Lincoln, Horace Greeley and George Fogg attended a special meeting of the Republican National Committee in Pittsburgh, prior to the 1856 Republican National Convention. Fogg was named to the executive committee of the new national party. In June, at the first Republican party convention in New Hampshire, held in Concord, Tuck called the sessions to order.

Amos Tuck led the New Hampshire delegation and served as a Vice President of the first Republican National Convention in Philadelphia. On the first ballot he persuaded eight of its members to vote for Abraham Lincoln for the office of Vice President. But it was Lewis William Dayton who won that nomination and, with John Charles Fremont as presidential nominee, they became the Republican ticket. The party lost the election to Democrat James Buchanan.

While campaigning for the Republicans in the 1856 campaign, Lincoln gave more than fifty speeches, but he avoided using the "Republican" name. Instead, he talked of "Fremont men" or "Anti-Nebraska" men. In New Hampshire a Fremont club was organized which adopted the slogan: "Free Speech, Free Men, Free States, and Fremont."

1859: Lincoln's son, Robert, had failed to qualify for admittance to Harvard. It was then that Abraham Lincoln decided to enroll him at Phillips Exeter Academy, where young Robert's concerted effort and improved preparation allowed his re-taking the entrance exams to Harvard, where he was admitted a year later.

According to a letter written by Edward Tuck, Amos's son, on March 28, 1935 (at age 93), Abraham Lincoln had gone to Exeter "to consult him (Amos Tuck) regarding the sending of his son to the Academy. At the time of his visit I was a student at Dartmouth college, and absent. Bob Lincoln himself came to Exeter later on, during my vacation, staying one night with us, and I well remember that I went with him the next day to find a boarding-house on the other side of the River, where he settled." — Letter from Exeter Historical Society Collections. Edward had just completed his own four years of study (1854-58) at Phillips Exeter Academy. [Editor's Note: This alleged visit by Lincoln conflicts with historical records. Historians generally deny that Lincoln was ever in Exeter in 1859.]

1860: During his 1860 presidential campaign, Lincoln definitely came to New Hampshire, giving speeches in Concord, Manchester, Dover and Exeter.

Lincoln did not visit Nashua, perhaps because of the attitude voiced by the Democratic *Nashua Gazette:* " 'Abe' Lincoln, of Ills., had been trotted round this state by the republicans during the past week. It is rumored, that he would have made a speech here, but he asked $100 for his services, and the Nashua Republicans considered him worth only half that sum. He is a dull, prosy speaker. A Republican who heard him at Providence, says, he would draw a big house, but two thirds of his audience would leave before he got through."

On March 3, 1860, Lincoln delivered his address to the students and townspeople at Exeter's Town Hall. Warren J. Prescott of Hampton, who attended the meeting, reported that Amos Tuck was seated on the platform. History professor Thomas C. Hayden of Phillips Exeter Academy alleges that Tuck joined his son Robert in saying "goodbye" to Lincoln at the Exeter train station when Lincoln departed on March 5th.

We know that Lincoln spent three nights in Exeter, and some historians, years later, recalled Tuck's being in Exeter also. However, Tuck himself, in a letter to Lincoln dated May 14, 1860, (found in the Library of Congress) wrote: "I very much regretted that I was absent when you were at Exeter, and was sorry you did not call upon my family, even in my absence."

Thus, there remains much speculation as to where Lincoln actually spent the three nights while in Exeter. In his *Abraham Lincoln in New Hampshire*, historian Elwin Page determined that "It is certain that Lincoln passed at least one night at the house of Amos Tuck at 89 Front Street."

There is also evidence that Lincoln spent one or more of the three nights at the Squamscot Hotel (formerly Blake's Hotel where the Party was founded) and/or in Bob's room at Mrs. Clark's boarding house, which accommodation Edward Tuck had procured as Bob's student residence. It was reliably reported that Abe proved himself a talented banjo player as he entertained his son's fellow students with college songs.

Whether or not Lincoln was a guest in the Tuck residence on this second Exeter visit, it is clear that the Tuck family was most hospitable to Robert Lincoln and thoughtfully concerned with his welfare. In Tuck's letter to Lincoln of May 14, 1860, he had also commented, "Your son was at my house, at tea, the evening before I left home (last Wednesday). He was in good health and

spirits, and I hope he will feel at home at my door while he remains in Exeter. He is a promising son."

Franklin Brooks, the biographer of Edward Tuck, noted that Robert stayed at "the Tucks' residence at Christmas for his parents could not afford to have him come home."

Mrs. Clark's boarding house *Exeter Historical Society*

Tuck's letter to Lincoln *Library of Congress*

Once again, in 1860, Amos Tuck led the New Hampshire delegation to the Second Republican Convention, in Chicago.

On May 14, in the same letter to Lincoln, previously-cited, Tuck explained his New Hampshire strategy to Lincoln:

My Dear Sir:

...I take great satisfaction in assuring you, that what I hoped might be practical, when I left home, seems to me when here, to be within the range of decided possibilities—I mean your nomination as President. I believe it is desirable for our party, and our principles, for you to be put on the track. I am taking hold of hands with our New England delegates, and find the prospect good for general cooperation. Be not misled by our first votes. It will be expedient not to strike at first, but to let the West make their first move. But we shall come in, 'on time.' In Phil., in 1856, I had the satisfaction, in the case of N.H., to name A.L. for Vice Pres., though I pretend not to have done much. If we can now put you up for Pres., in cooperation with your other friends, I shall have confidence that we are acting wisely for the country, and you shall have our prayers for success and long life.

Amos Tuck

On the first ballot at the Convention, seven of New Hampshire's ten delegates voted for Lincoln. It was the only New England state to cast a majority vote for him. Due to Tuck's leadership, all New Hampshire delegates voted for him on the third and decisive vote. Thus, five days after Tuck's letter, Abraham Lincoln was named the standard bearer of the Republican Party...although the candidate himself was not in attendance.

Tuck was one of a committee chosen to wait upon him in Springfield, Illinois, to announce Lincoln's nomination to him and receive his acceptance.

I do not know that any member of the company, other than Mr. Tuck of New Hampshire, and some of the Western men, had ever seen him (Lincoln) before, but there was that about him which commanded instant admiration," wrote Charles Carleton Coffin, western correspondent of the Boston Journal.
—*The Lincoln Reader, by Paul M. Angle, 1947*

After remaining in Lincoln's home for a few hours, the committee adjoined to a ratification meeting at the Illinois State House, where Amos Tuck was one of those chosen to address the gathering.

"Tuck's intimacy with the Lincolns was so close that he accompanied Mrs. Lincoln on the occasion of her shopping tour in New York before the inauguration," wrote Elwin Page, although Franklin Brooks differed with Page on this particular incident. Brooks agreed with Page that Lincoln had spent an overnight as a guest at the Tuck home.

Mrs. Lincoln and Mrs. Tuck were frequent correspondents, and the Tucks were welcomed visitors to the White House. The two fathers kindly reciprocated in their care and concern for their sons, i.e. Robert Lincoln and Edward Tuck, at various stages of their youth.

NEW REPUBLICAN PARTY
ADOPTS TUCK'S PRINCIPLES

Tuck's leadership was evident, his handprint was every-where… specifically and most assuredly, as he was elected a vice president of the 1856 Republican National Convention in Philadelphia and had influenced its platform committee, then served on that same committee at Chicago in 1860.

The platform of principles adopted on both occasions was based on Tuck's own resolutions presented to the Convention which he had led in Exeter on February 22, 1845. He avers to this himself in his *Exeter News-Letter* **Article No. IX of September 1, 1876:**

> **In fact there was no utterance by the New Hampshire Independent Democrats of 1845 which had to be modified in any degree, in order to comport with the positions assumed by the great Republican party, when it came into being, eleven years afterward. From 1845 to 1856, the Independents, with varying successes in New Hampshire, kept up the fight and gradually progressed in combining with all good men who would join them, and especially with the Whig party, whose members generally acted towards them with great generosity and with due regard to the good of the country, until the fullness of their time when the great Republican party was formed, which saved the Government and the Union, and purified and perpetuated our institutions.**

Tuck was seriously considered by Lincoln for a position in the President's Cabinet. Instead, he accepted a prestigious presidential appointment as naval officer of the Port of Boston, where he remained until ousted by Andrew Johnson, Democratic president who began his four-year term in 1865. He was appointed as a prominent delegate to the "Peace Congress" in 1861.

From 1840 to 1853, the Tuck family lived at 72 Front Street *Exeter Historical Society*

ABRAHAM LINCOLN

President of the United · States of America.

To all to whom these Presents shall come, Greeting:

KNOW YE, That, reposing special trust and confidence in the Integrity, Diligence and Discretion of

Amos Tuck

I have Nominated, and by and with the advice and consent of the Senate, **DO APPOINT HIM**
Naval Officer for the District of Boston and Charlestown, in the State of Massachusetts,
and do authorize and empower him to execute and fulfil the duties of that Office, according to law; **AND TO HAVE AND TO HOLD,**
the said Office with all the rights and emoluments thereunto legally appertaining, unto him, the said Amos Tuck
during the term of four years from the 14th day of March, 1861, unless this Commission be sooner revoked by the President
of the United · States for the time being.

IN TESTIMONY WHEREOF, I have caused these Letters to be made Patent and the Seal of the
Treasury Department of the United · States to be hereunto affixed.
Given under my hand, at the City of Washington the sixteenth day of March
in the year of our Lord one thousand eight hundred and sixty one, and of the Independence
of the United States of America the eighty fifth —

By the President: Abraham Lincoln

S P Chase, Secretary of the Treasury

Tuck's appointment by Lincoln *Baker Library at Dartmouth*

Abraham Lincoln

President of the United States of America,

TO ALL TO WHOM THESE PRESENTS SHALL COME, GREETING:

Know ye, That, reposing special trust and confidence in the integrity, diligence, and discretion of *Amos Tuck*

I DO APPOINT HIM *Naval Officer for the District of Boston and Charlestown, in the State of Massachusetts,* and do authorize and empower him to execute and fulfil the duties of that office according to law; and to have and to hold the said office, with all the rights and emoluments thereunto legally appertaining, unto him, the said *Amos Tuck* during the pleasure of the PRESIDENT OF THE UNITED STATES for the time being, and until the end of the next session of the Senate of the United States, and no longer.

In testimony whereof, I have caused these Letters to be made Patent, and the Seal of the Treasury Department of the United States to be hereunto affixed.

Given under my hand, at the CITY OF WASHINGTON, this *fourteenth* day of *March* in the year of Our Lord one thousand eight hundred and *sixty five* and of the INDEPENDENCE OF THE UNITED STATES OF AMERICA the *eighty ninth.*

BY THE PRESIDENT:

Abraham Lincoln

Hugh McCulloch
Secretary of the Treasury.

10

Re-appointed

Tuck's re-appointment by Lincoln *Baker Library at Dartmouth*

DID LINCOLN'S VISIT TO EXETER IN 1860 MAKE HIM PRESIDENT?

"Did Lincoln's Visit to Exeter in 1860 Make Him President?" asked Edgar Warren, in a *Boston Evening Transcript* feature dated October 29, 1927.

During the late 1850's, the Democratic party was in continuing disarray, largely because the "Little Giant," Stephen A. Douglas, had split the Democratic party from top to bottom. The Republicans thought this gave them a good chance of winning. Their likely candidate was Senator William H. Seward of New York, who was internationally known and in a position of "commanding influence."

Except for the debates with Douglas, Lincoln was relatively unknown in the Northeast. Though he had been a U.S. Congressman, he was basically a country lawyer and a man of meager means.

It was not until he was offered an expense-paid trip and honorarium from the Young Men's Central Republican Union of New York City that he saw his chance to visit the Northeast. He seized the offer largely because it provided him with the opportunity of visiting his son at Exeter, as part of a speaking tour both in New York and New England. "The desire to visit Robert at his school, not the ambition to forward his own fortunes, was clearly the chief motive for accepting the invitation to make an address in the East," wrote Elwin Page.

Lincoln gave one of the most outstanding speeches of his fledgling career at the Cooper Union of New York City, before going to Exeter. The trip turned out to be one of the most fortuitous moves of his campaign:

> In March 1860 former Illinois Congressman Abraham Lincoln visited New Hampshire, made triumphant speeches, and suddenly became a leading candidate for the Presidency.
> —**Ronald & Grace Jager**, *History of the Granite State, 1983.*

Warren speculated that if Lincoln had not made the trip, he would have remained a "shadowy figure" to New England voters, and their support would logically have gone to Seward. At the Chicago Convention, it was the "rush" of New Hampshire and the northern New England delegates on the second ballot, directed by Amos Tuck, that caused the "stampede" on the third ballot that won Lincoln the nomination.

Even Lincoln's son Robert, in later years, said that his "abysmal flunk" at Harvard in 1859 made his father president. His attending Phillips Exeter Academy had brought his father to New Hampshire and New England, a region whose leadership eventually assured Abraham Lincoln's nomination.

Warren also recounts an incident that occurred when William Howard Taft, after his retirement from the presidency, addressed the students at Phillips Exeter Academy. The former president was introduced by Professor James A. Tufts, who proffered that Lincoln never would have been President if his son had not attended the Academy. Taft had responded, "My great regret is that I had not heard this story several years ago, for if I had I would have sent my son Charlie to the Academy before I ran for President the second time."

AMOS TUCK, A PRE-EMINENT CITIZEN

Tuck's fine appearance, personal charm, and public spirit gave him a prominent place in that group of lawyers and party leaders which made Exeter one of the influential centers of New England life in the nineteenth century.

—*Dictionary of American Biography*

Said Franklin Brooks

He (Joseph G. Hoyt) and Amos were the principal proponents of building Exeter a new Town Hall in the early 1850's where Lincoln gave his campaign speech in 1860....Tuck and Atty. Henry Flagg French adopted a motion to plant the streets of Exeter with elm trees.

Amos Tuck was a Trustee of Phillips Exeter Academy for nearly thirty years, and of Dartmouth College for ten. He was a trustee and benefactor of the Robinson Seminary.

After serving five years at his post in Boston, Tuck went to work for the Atlantic & Pacific railroads, lived in St. Louis for a time, traveled extensively and visited Europe, always maintaining his Front Street residence in Exeter, where he died.

———◆———

Amos lived at 89 Front Street, in Exeter, for 26 years, from 1853 when the house was built, until his death. His dedication to the town was self-avowed, demonstrated by his continual involvement and several specific contributions—some less significant than others, but all of them lasting.

Amos Tuck's home at 89 Front Street *Exeter Historical Society*

TUCK SPEAKS FOR HIMSELF

Amos Tuck spoke eloquently for himself, though he was notably modest when it came to acknowledgment of his own singular accomplishments. His devotion to principle, to the Republican movement he founded, and to the State of New Hampshire, however, are clearly articulated in his own personal writings and numerous speeches.

Said John P. Hale:

> Hon. Amos Tuck…at Downer's Landing in 1878, met the claim of Massachusetts that the Republican party was founded there in 1848, by showing that that party was anticipated in everyone of its ideas by the Hale party in New Hampshire in 1845.
>
> —*John P. Hale by William E. Chandler, 1892.*

Amos Speaks…

At Downer's Landing on August 9, 1878, to a group of Massachusetts Republicans commemorating their own "founding" of the Republican Party:

In 1845 we made a declaration of principles that constituted the essence of the Republican party which was formed at Philadelphia eleven years later….

You have no right, permit me to say, to write on the page of history that the republican enterprise in this country began in 1848. Previous to 1848, I have told you how we organized the opposition in New Hampshire in 1845. We began in 1844…and in the revolution that took place in the United States, bear in mind that the humble state of New Hampshire placed the first anti-slavery senator in the Senate of the United States.

While we cannot claim much in our little State, we are very jealous of what little we can claim. I say that here are the declarations carefully made at that Exeter meeting, where we published an address and resolutions, and we had no occasion, up to the time of the formation of the Republican party, and in all our labors in the Republican party, and in all our votes in Congress or out, to cross a 't' or dot an 'i' of what we wrote in February 1845. And there is the document! Your patent was not taken out until 1848.

1875
FROM AMOS TUCK'S
OWN AUTOBIOGRAPHY

Referring to the movement of 1844–45:

Thus began the first successful protest and rebellion in the Democratic party, against the pro-slavery action of that party, whichever took place in the United States. Its origin was humble, and it was my fortune to be at the fountain, influential in the inception of a movement which soon agitated the whole country, controlled parties, created the Republican Party, and finally saved the government. I hesitate to declare, even to my children, the leading part which I took in directing the incipient measures which eventuated in expelling slavery from the country. Our movement in New Hampshire antedated by about two years, and promoted the movement of, the 'conscious Whigs' of Massachusetts, led by Henry Wilson, John G. Palfrey, Charles, and Charles Francis Adams, and for a longer period, preceded the 'Barnburner' organization of New York, in which Martin Van Buren and others participated. The newspapers of those years will confirm the statement that the action of the 'Independent Democrats' of New Hampshire inaugurated successful political anti-slavery action inside of one of the great political parties, and taught conscientious men in all parts of the country that it was possible to sustain themselves by appeals to the honor and conscience of the people.

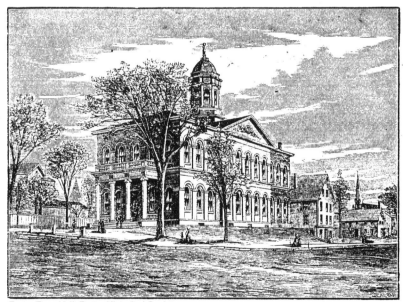

Exeter Town Hall *Exeter Historical Society*

TUCK BEGINS IMPORTANT COLUMN SERIES

On February 18, 1876, Amos Tuck began a series of historical recollections about the uprising of the "Independent Democracy" in New Hampshire, pursuant to a request from the *Exeter News-Letter*. In the introduction to the series, the editor said:

> **Upon the foundations laid by Mr. Tuck and his colleagues was built the great Free Soil party, which afterwards took the name Republican.**

In Tuck's first article, called "Independent Democracy in New Hampshire," he wrote:

> **...the union between New Hampshire Whigs and Independent Democrats introduced and inaugurated the combinations which in 1856 resulted in the organization of the Republican party at Philadelphia upon a platform, identical in its chief features, with the issue raised in New Hampshire eleven years before.**

Reproduction of the complete articles has been acquired from the original *Exeter News-Letters*. They are lengthy and the print is very fine, which is why only excerpts are reprinted here.

In Article III:

> Not till after a little band of independent voters in New Hampshire had raised the standard of revolt, and triumphed under that standard, did there seem to be even the breath of life in all the dissatisfied elements of the Democratic party, outside the Granite State. Mr. Van Buren and his followers took courage from our success and in 1848 did what was done by us in 1845. The men who were indignant with Henry Clay in 1844, held fast to their party till they witnessed the success of our appeal to the people, when they came to the rescue, and the new combinations commenced which ultimately constituted the Republican party.

In Article XI:

Tuck pays tribute to his long-time friend and newspaper editor, George G. Fogg, on September 15, 1876:

> ...the history of Independent Democracy in New Hampshire, and likewise of Republicanism, through all the stages of its great trials, to the time of its final accession to power, includes the history of Mr. Fogg's labors, in the ranks of those who did most for the honor of the State and the welfare of the nation. For sixteen years, the *Independent Democrat* was under his sole control and immediate supervision, and exerted an ever-extending influence in the state and the country. **It advocated Republicanism for eleven years before the Republican party came into being,** and it never took a position during the history of its varied work, which time and experience have not vindicated as wise, patriotic and statesmanlike. In 1861 Mr. Fogg was selected by Mr. Lincoln to represent our Government in Switzerland, which position he held with honor, until 1867, when he returned to America. Resuming his labors as editor, he conducted the *Independent Democrat* for some years with his usual ability and success, until the period arrived, when in contemplation of the great work achieved for the whole country, in which he had taken so conspicuous a part, he felt himself at liberty to retire; whereupon the Independent Democrat became united with the *New Hampshire Statesman*, taking the name of the *Independent Statesman*, under which title it is now published."

Unfortunately, Mr. Tuck became very ill and was unable to conclude the series. The *Exeter News-Letter* kept its readers advised of the state of his health, always hoping he would continue his valuable account of the history he had helped to create.

Amos Tuck died suddenly at his home in Exeter on December 11, 1879, at the age of sixty-nine. He is buried in the cemetery of the town he loved so well.

Thus, it was left to his friends and acquaintances, such as the Rev. Jeremiah W. Dearborn of Parsonsfield, to memorialize his accomplishments.

On December 26, 1879, the editor of the *Exeter News-Letter*, wrote the following, urging continuation of Tuck's columns by his colleague, John L. Hayes:

> We hope Mr. Hayes will be persuaded to give a more extensive narrative of the events that led to the formation of the 'Independent Democracy' of New Hampshire, the vanguard of the great party that afterwards put down a mighty rebellion and struck the shackles from four millions of slaves. Boston has been appropriately named the cradle of liberty because there was nursed the spirit of the revolution; **history will yet do equal justice to Exeter where was kindled a flame that could not be stayed until it had purged the nation of the last trace of oppression.... When the full history of the Republican party comes to be written it will be made known that it was born and cradled here in Exeter, and nurtured by sincere and patriotic men, without desire or hope of reward....The little meeting in Exeter on the 22d of February, 1845, emancipated political opinion in New Hampshire, and the noble infection spread quickly to Maine and throughout New England....Four millions of slaves were made freemen as the result of that little meeting at the court house in Exeter on an inclement day in the winter of 1845.**

In 1885, John Lord Hayes' *A Reminiscence of the Free-Soil Movement in New Hampshire, 1845*, was published. He refers to the letter that appeared in the *Exeter News-Letter* on the day of Amos Tuck's death, December 12, 1879, which had been jointly prepared by Amos Tuck and himself, the very day before Tuck died. Long passages from that letter were used in the memorial discourse on Mr. Tuck which was delivered by Rev. George E. Street at Exeter, New Hampshire on January 11, 1880. Excerpts of the eulogy follow.

TUCK REMEMBERED

"HERE, IN EXETER..."

On January 11, 1880, at a memorial service for Amos Tuck in the Second Congregational Church of Exeter, the Rev. George E. Street referred to the February 22, 1845 meeting:

> Why have I given this political incident such prominence here? For two reasons: the first is because of its historic importance. In that little body of resolute men, gathered, I think, in the vestry of the old First Church of this town, was the first crystallized opposition to the extension of the slaveholders' role in the land,—the nucleus of that great party, which, ten years afterwards, became national and has made history so rapidly.
>
> It was fitting that here in Exeter, where on the 23rd of May, 1775, the Colonial Legislature anticipated the Bill of Rights, which occurred on the fourth day of July, 1776, because 'the Declaration by Thirteen States of their independence,' the keynote of liberty, should again be sounded in advance, to the rest of the nation."
>
> —*"A Memorial Discourse" by Rev. George E. Street, Franklin Press, Rand Avery & Co., 1880, Boston.*

The same pamphlet included a tribute to Amos Tuck, written by A.P. Peabody, President of Board of Trustees, on behalf of Phillips Exeter Academy, dated December 11, 1879. The resolution would appear in the records of P.E.A., Cambridge, December 24, 1879.

From the *Sketch of the Life and Character of Hon. Amos Tuck*, read before the Maine Historical Society, by Jeremiah W. Dearborn, M.D., of Parsonsfield, Maine in 1888, published in his biography in 1904:

> That the claim here made for Mr. Tuck that he was the first man to begin the organization of what became later the Republican party is just, I take the liberty to make the following extract from a speech which he made on the occasion of a "Reunion of the Freesoilers of 1848," held at Downer's Landing, Hingham, Mass., on August 9, 1877. Mr. Charles Francis Adams, who was called to preside at that meeting, made an address in which he claimed that the Free Soil party of this country originated in Massachusetts in 1848. Mr. Tuck in reference thereto said, 'Now, you are making up history here, and nobody can make up history better, or that is likely to last longer, than the people of Massachusetts; but will you please to take account of things that happened prior to 1848. Will you not bear in mind Mr. Adams, and gentlemen, that two years before, and more than two years previous to that date, people in the state of New Hampshire set an example of a conflict with party leaders that had never been set in this country before? [Applause.] We organized an opposition to the Democratic party in 1844-45, which we have never given up to this day. [Renewed applause.] And in 1845 we made a declaration of principles that constituted the essence of the Republican party, which was formed at Philadelphia eleven years later.

Tuck biographer Jeremiah W. Dearborn was a friend of the Tuck family and of John Tuck, Amos' brother, specifically. John was of particular assistance and encouragement to J.W. Dearborn, upon his writing of the prodigious *History of the First Century of the Town of Parsonsfield, Maine,* published by Brown, Thurston, & Co., Portland, Maine, 1888. This extensive work establishes Dearborn as a biographer/historian of indisputable repute.

------◆------

In 1842 Mr. Tuck was representative in the New Hampshire legislature, and took an active part in the revision of the statutes enacted that year. He was a democrat in politics, but in 1844 he separated from the party with others, on the pro-slavery measure of the annexation of Texas, and in 1846 was nominated by the Independent Democrats for a member of Congress, and in 1847, by a combination of the Independent Democrats with the Whigs, **was elected to Congress, where he took his seat in December of that year, as one of the only three distinctively anti-slavery men in the national House of Representatives.** These men were Joshua R. Giddings of Ohio, Dr. John G. Palfrey of Massachusetts, and Amos Tuck of New Hampshire. Hon. John P. Hale, of New Hampshire, was the only anti-slavery senator in the higher branch of Congress.

The declaration of principles on which the Independents and the Whigs of New Hampshire united in 1846–47, and their union of action, was the first movement towards the formation of the great Republican party, which was eventually organized in Philadelphia in 1856, which nominated Mr. Lincoln at Chicago in 1860, carried the country in the election of that year, and eventually saved the government in the great struggle from 1861 to 1865.

Mr. Tuck was a member of the committee at the convention in Philadelphia, which gave the name of Republican to the new party, and which reported the platform of declared principles, a portion of which was drawn up by himself, on which the organization rallied. He was likewise a member of the Chicago Convention in 1860, and advocated from the first the nomination of Mr. Lincoln, whom he had previously known in Congress; and again as member of the Platform Committee at that convention, aided in the formation of the declaration of principles on which the great party rallied and were victorious in the election of Mr. Lincoln.

—*Robert Tuck, of Hampton, N.H. and his Descendants, by Joseph Dow, 1877.*

------◆------

The most complete account of Amos Tuck's prominence and leadership in establishing the Republican Party came from Dr. D. Homer Batchelder, who attended the meeting of October 12, 1853. His letter, often referred to by supporting authors, follows.

The Republican Party

NEW HAMPSHIRE CLAIMS TO BE ITS BIRTH-PLACE AND AMOS TUCK THE FIRST TO NAME IT. HOW HORACE GREELEY FIRST LEARNED ABOUT IT.

EDITOR EXETER NEWS-LETTER.—

During the last three or four years there has been quite a little contest between citizens of several states in relation to the birth-place of the Republican party. At one time the Citizens of the town of Strong, in Maine, claimed that the party was born there. Others in the state of New York also assert that they took part in the par-turient, and also in the nursing ceremonies at the time, and after the Republican child first saw the light; while a like claim has been put forth by members of the party in Massachusetts, Vermont, and Minnesota. Now, I wish, if possible, to avoid every appearance of a controversy in the matter, but in order that this matter shall be based on facts which may give to it a correct status in the future history of the party, I must be allowed to say, that none of those who have thus far claimed to be its "God Father" are quite correct.

During the war with Mexico, the result of which was the annex-ation of Texas, and from its close down to 1853, all political parties in New Hampshire excepting the Democratic, seemed to be in a fusing condition; in fact everybody seemed to be "waiting for something to turn up." During those troublesome years of incuba-tion, New Hampshire had hatched out two additional parties, and there had come to be five distinct political parties, viz.: the regular Democratic organization, which has held political control of the state for a long series of years; and opposed to that the Whig party, the old original abolition Hoyt and Garrison party, the Free-Soil party, and the Independent Democratic party, which was led by such men as George G. Fogg, John P. Hale and Amos Tuck. The latter was called forth in consequence of the annexation of Texas and was made up of dissenting Democrats who followed John P. Hale when he left the Democratic party and was joined by Amos Tuck and Fogg, with many other leading Democrats of the state.

To obtain a united action of the four parties was no small task. By a close and accurate canvass we found that by a complete and united vote of the four parties against the Democrats, we could elect state officers and possibly the Legislature. But, what a task! All of the committees must be consulted and a large number of the leading men were to be reconciled to united status. It looked formidable and, at first, scarcely possible. But we went to work—and we did work as men never worked before—and at the annual meeting in March, 1847, the crucible was emptied, and, to the surprise of all, the fusion had carried the election of the Legislature with a majority of three only, while there was no choice by the people of state officers, a hopeful result. June came, and the Legislature was organized by the fusionists by electing John P. Hale speaker of the house. Gen. Anthony Colby, the Whig candidate for Governor, was elected to that office while the other state offices were filled by worthy men from the different parties.

The term of John P. Hale as a member of Congress had closed on the fourth of March previous, and his head was cut off by the Democrats because he had opposed the annexation of Texas. He was elected on joint ballot a United States Senator for six years to take the place of Charles G. Atherton, whose term had expired. But, notwithstanding these grand results, the old Whig leaders ("who were dyed in the wool") were slow to give up their old party organizations, which they declared must be kept intact. They were

headed by Ichabod Bartlett and Ichabod Goodwin, of Portsmouth; Daniel M. Christy and Thomas E. Sawyer, of Dover; Asa McFarland and Judge Perley, of Concord; Wilson and Chamberlain, of Keene, &c. And so we struggled on as best we could under separate organizations, till Mr. Webster (with hopes exhausted) died; and then the end came; and the several parties, co-workers under separate banners until this time, 1852, saw the folly of continuing their political labors for the one and same purpose under an all but chaotic segregation. The subject began to increase in interest and in a manner to invite a general discussion.

About this time, by whom I do not know, an organization sprang into existence; it is sufficient to say that its starting point was farther south than New England. In this, an attempt was made to build up an organization known and recognized as the American party; and very soon was prefixed to its name an adjective by which it was known as the Know-Nothing American party.

The voters of New Hampshire did not become very strongly attached to that unique system of politics, but rather sought something higher—more ennobling and enduring. Consequently there arose a feeling in Rockingham County especially, early in fifty-three, that steps must be taken to secure a more perfect union of the four parties, if we would secure the attainment of the high and grand results aimed at in the advanced steps already taken by these segmentary organizations. The writer had frequently communicated with Mr. Tuck, Mr. Fogg, Mr. Young, of Portsmouth, and McFarland, with others, of the necessity of adopting a more permanent and united action, and also with regards to the means by which it might be brought about. And here, I might say that in the first Congressional district (Rockingham county) we had secured an almost uninterrupted union in the election of Mr. Tuck two or three times to Congress.

During the month of September 1853, I received at Londonderry (my native town) a note from Mr. Tuck, of which I append a copy:

Exeter, Sept. 28th, 1853

My dear sir:—We deem it advisable to hold an informal meeting, composed of some of the principal members of the parties, at this place, on the 12th of October (Wednesday) at Major Blake's Hotel. One of the principal objects of this informal meeting is to fix on a plan of harmonizing the different party organizations, whereby a more united co-operation can be secured and the four parties may pull together under one title of organization. Hale, McFarland and Fogg will be present. We shall expect you and Currier, of Auburn, to be present.

Yours Respectfully,

Amos Tuck

I attended that meeting and am made to feel sorrowful when I am called to advert to the long ago assemblage of that little, but very important gathering, which took place almost unknown to anyone but ourselves. It was composed of fourteen persons, all told, counting Major Blake, who took part. And who can wonder that the writer feels sad when obliged to say, that thirteen out of the number have long passed to that bourne from which no one returns! Their work on earth is done, and the writer is left alone to tell the tale. Their names were as follows, as near as I can recollect: John P. Hale, Amos Tuck, Mr. Blake, I. Bartlett, Hackett, McFarland, George Fogg, David Currier, Plummer, Young, Preston, with two I cannot recall—and myself.

It was at and during the informal session of that meeting that Hon. Amos Tuck, of Exeter, proposed that we use our influence to the end that all the political organizations, who had rather informally acted together thus far in behalf of one general object, should drop individual titles and hereafter be known and recognized as one party, under one common title, and that the name, "Republican" be prefixed to the party and that it be hereafter known as the Republican party. Mr. Tuck argued, "that this name would seem to convey its principles, and would be more likely to become nationalized, be significant of a great national party in process of time." After a friendly exchange of opinion, it was agreed then and there, to use our individual influences to bring about and have established that important change as soon as it could be done harmoniously. And we separated, never to meet again on such an occasion. And let me say, that there was no record kept of this meeting, no reporter allowed to be present, and no notice ever printed. I saw Mr. Tuck frequently after this meeting took place, and he was very zealous in the work of organizing and consolidating the party. He was worthy of the confidence of every member of it.

Now again, during the month of December, 1853, Horace Greeley made his annual visit to his old home at Londonderry, spending a week or so. The fact that it was my native town and that we had been boys together gave us lasting ties through life. During his visit as above stated, we spent a part of the day together, and during our conversation, I related to him confidentially what had taken place at Exeter the October before; but, as it was confidentially informal, I did not wish him to name it in the Tribune. "But," said he, "I think it will be necessary to adopt some general name, and I think Republican would be the best name; it will sound both Jeffersonian and Madisonian, and for that reason will take well." Horace returned to New York and I kept along in the work of my profession, and before the dawn of 1854, we in that part of New Hampshire were known by the title of Republicans.

Now then, I read from the New York Tribune, issued August 8th, 1884, a paragraph as a portion of a letter from one A. N. Cole. It read thus: "Horace Greeley named the party in a letter to myself in 1854, sometime in the month of April. The letter was published in the *Genesee Valley Free Press,* the pioneer Republican journal of America."

I do not entertain a doubt that Mr. Cole's report of what Mr. Greeley did and said is correct, so far as his letter is concerned. But it in no sense establishes the fact that Horace Greeley was the original author or gave to the great Republican party its name. I can aver with certainty that in December preceding the time of his writing this letter to Mr. Cole, in April, 1854, he knew nothing of a new and established party by the Republican name. In my conversation with him at that time (in December) the American Know-Nothing party was involved in an experiment, and its movements were quite keenly watched by Mr. Greeley. He had been a Clay Whig with anti-slavery tendencies — wrote and acted as such, till the death of Mr. Clay and after; and sometime after Mr. Webster had been deposited in the tomb, in the autumn of 1853, he had not identified himself with the fortunes of any new party that had not permanent title or name. Even at the time I conversed with him about the subject, he considered it rather Utopian, and only lent his assent, without pledging his support in any way. So I can easily imagine that he kept the subject under consideration until the next April and had so far been favorably impressed as to "look upon it" as a possibility, if not an established reality. Hence, the letter to Mr. Cole.

Knowing these facts as I do, from his own lips, I have no doubt that his convictions were such as to write the letter with due propriety, in the April of 1854, after due deliberation upon the lesson he had learned in New Hampshire many months before. But the name of the great national party (Republican) was first suggested and introduced as early as the autumn of 1853. And, so far as I have any knowledge of the suggestion and practical application, it came from the Hon. Amos Tuck of Exeter, New Hampshire, in 1853.

D. Homer Batchelder
Danversport, Mass.

SON, EDWARD TUCK, REMEMBERED WELL

In one of the tributes made to Amos Tuck during a commemorative event in 1929, Albertus T. Dudley revealed that he had received a letter from Edward Tuck, son of Amos, in which Edward had responded to Dudley's query about the October 12th meeting:

I recall his (Amos) having spoken to me of that meeting, as well as of others, and his saying that the name 'Republican' had appealed to him as the proper one for the new national party which he felt sure was bound to be formed and regularly organized by the anti-slavery men throughout the country. He said he had proposed it at the meeting in October, 1853, and that he had written to Horace Greeley, suggesting the name.

"There is no doubt that the rebellion against the Democratic party in New Hampshire and the different meetings in Exeter, were the foundation stone of the Republican Party and that to Exeter is due the credit of first proposing the name," wrote Tuck.

Dudley added: **Amos Tuck must be considered not alone one of the important founders of the Republican party, but the first prophet to herald its coming.**

QUOTES FROM OTHERS WHO HAVE SUPPORTED THE TUCK/EXETER CLAIM

Charles Robert Corning, *Amos Tuck*, Exeter, NH, The *News-Letter Press*, 1902:

> **He had accomplished much with few tools; he was now to accomplish more with implements better adapted to the work. He had conferred lasting distinction on his state and his name has the right to be carved with that of John P. Hale as New Hampshire's earliest champion of the cause of human freedom. He was now to perform an act which entitled him to historical remembrance. If not Amos Tuck, who was the man that gave the name republican to the forces gathering to resist slavery? As a Free-Soiler, the evidence is conclusive as to his priority of action regarding anti-slavery, nor is evidence wanting to prove his early action respected the party name of Republican.**

Jonathan Pecker, 1838–1915,

A noted biographer who wrote sketches on several political figures of that era, including those on Amos Tuck and George G. Fogg.

Of Tuck's influence, he said:

> **The combination to elect these two men to Congress, completed in New Hampshire the work of forming a new party, which had begun when Mr. Hale was elected to the Senate in 1846. This combination was how the Republican party, first begun in New Hampshire, nine years before like combinations in other states, assembled in Convention in Philadelphia in 1856, triumphant in the Granite State on declaration of principles identical with those adopted at Philadelphia, when the principles and the name Republican were adopted and proclaimed.**

In Elwin Page's *Abraham Lincoln in New Hampshire*, 1929, the circumstances of the October 1853 meeting are clearly described:

> In 1853, things seemed to be in an impasse. Tuck was out of Congress. Wilson had removed to California. Hale could not be reelected. The most that was possible was to keep the Legislature from electing a Senator, but the Democrats again had the Governor and he made an appointment.
>
> Then Tuck conceived the bold idea of uniting all of the anti-slavery elements of the State—Whig, Independent Democrat, Free-Soil, Know-Nothing—into a new party. In October, 1853, he got together secretly in Exeter thirteen other men, including, besides Hale and Fogg, Asa McFarland, the Whig leader of Concord. Tuck suggested that all party names be dropped and that the four factions unite under the name Republican. His suggestion was unanimously approved, and thus was projected the first Republican Party in any State.

In his article on Lincoln in New Hampshire, Thomas C. Hayden, too, concurred that when in Exeter, Lincoln had visited with Amos Tuck, a former Democrat and now a "new" Republican. With John Parker Hale, the first man ever elected to Congress on an antislave ticket, Tuck and twelve others had founded the Republican Party in Major Blake's Hotel on the corner of Front and Court Streets, where Gorham Hall now stands.

In addressing the Amos Tuck Society at its first annual meeting, held at the Exeter Inn on October 12, 1994, New Hampshire historian, James L. Garvin, said, "I haven't been able to learn that anyone can prove an earlier meeting....For this reason, I conclude that the Republican party was truly born in Major Blake's tavern here in Exeter October 12, 1853."

15 AVENUE DES FLEURS
MONTE-CARLO

March 28th, 1935.

Dear Miss Diman:-

I have received your letter of 6th instant, but have been prevented by over occupation from replying to your question sooner.   Yes, Mr. Lincoln slept at my father's house, having come to Exeter to consult him regarding the sending of his son Robert to the Academy, which he afterwards did.   It was the house now occupied by my niece, Laura Nelson, my father having built and moved into it in the years 1852/3.   At the time of his visit I was a student at Dartmouth College, and absent. Bob Lincoln himself came to Exeter later on, during my vacation, staying one night with us, and I well remember that I went with him the next day to find a boarding-house on the other side of the river, where he settled.   I think I have in Paris a little book in which more particulars of these events are printed. If I find it I will send it to you after my return North in May or June.

I feel complimented that my photograph and letter should have been thought worthy of being hung in the upper entrance hall of the High School.   I regret that my present age prevents the possibility of my ever visiting Exeter again and seeing the many improvements that have been made in the town.

Miss Laura Nelson is at Mentone, only five or six miles away from me, and I see her constantly.   She was interested in your letter, and wishes me to send you her kind remembrances. We have had a very mild winter here as compared with yours at home, which she fortunately has escaped.   Her health is much improved.

Believe me,

Yours sincerely,

Edward Tuck

Letter from Edward Tuck to Miss Diman, March 28, 1935 *Exeter Historical Society*

THE FRENCH CONNECTION

Exeter News-Letter "Town Affairs" December 19, 1879:

> D.C. (Daniel Chester) French, the artist, was in town last Friday and took a cast for a bust of the late Hon. Amos Tuck. A portrait of Mr. Tuck in oil will soon be added to the Academy collection.

This original bust of Amos Tuck can be seen at the New Hampshire State Library in Concord. It was presented by his daughter, Ellen (Mrs. Francis O. French) and rendered by one of America's greatest classical sculptors, New Hampshire's own Daniel Chester French, a native of Exeter, who was a cousin of Francis O. French.

Margaret French Cresson, daughter of Daniel C. French, wrote about her grandfather, Henry Flagg French, and the elm trees he and Amos Tuck had designated for the streets of Exeter in her *Journey into Fame: The Life of Daniel Chester French*. Her survey of her father's works mentions portraits of Amos Tuck and Francis O. French, Tuck's son-in-law.

Amos' son Edward and Daniel Chester French collaborated as patron-artist in the creation of the New Hampshire Historical Society headquarters in Concord, and on several other occasions.

Attorney Henry Flagg French of Exeter was the father of Daniel Chester French, and a close friend of Amos Tuck and Joseph G. Hoyt. Henry's brother, Benjamin Brown French, was the father of Francis O. French (also called Frank), who married Tuck's daughter Ellen.

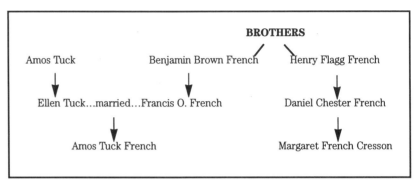

Amos and Henry Flagg French were close friends & law partners.

It is noteworthy that Benjamin Brown French, a prominent figure in his own right and father-in-law of Amos' daughter Ellen, knew a great deal about the Tuck-Hale movement from his brother, Henry, and wrote frequently of his close relationship with and admiration for Amos Tuck.

Benjamin Brown French had been a close, old friend of Franklin Pierce who had worked hard for his nomination and election as President. He saw him often in Washington, where they enjoyed horseback riding together and several convivial visits. Pierce appointed B.B. French Commissioner of Public Buildings with duties beginning July 1, 1853.

Benjamin frequently saw his brother Henry, who often left the cold winters of Exeter to stay with Benjamin in Washington. During his stay the winter of 1854, both were very disturbed by Pierce's support of the Kansas-Nebraska bill. Henry made no secret of his opposition to that controversial bill, whereupon Franklin Pierce beckoned Benjamin to the White House to warn him that his brother's strong views were injuring him politically, inferring that Henry's views might well have been reflective of Ben's.

Soon after, Benjamin Brown French's long friendship with Pierce ended, over the slavery issue, and by 1856, Benjamin had become a Republican, went to the Republican Convention and helped nominate Fremont. In 1861, he would be re-appointed as Commissioner of Public Buildings, this time as a Republican, by President Abraham Lincoln with whom, through Amos Tuck, had emerged a friendly acquaintance.

In *Witness to the Young Republic, A Yankee's Journal, 1828-1870,* Benjamin Brown French's diary and collection of letters, editors Donald B. Cole and John J. McDonough relate the following: "When (Benjamin) French visited Henry Flagg French (his brother & friend of Amos Tuck) in Exeter in 1855, he was entertained by Amos Tuck, **who had recently organized the Republican party in New Hampshire** and would soon be a force behind Abraham Lincoln. French also met Tuck's daughter Ellen, who later married Frank.

B.B. French's love of politics makes his journal a storehouse of political information. Family ties made him the confidant of Amos Tuck, a founder of the Republican party in New Hampshire. French, along with Tuck, enjoyed several visits to the Lincolns in the White House.

In August of 1858, B.B. French learned from Mr. Tuck that John Greenleaf Whittier was in Exeter, and had been at Tuck's house. Tuck accompanied French to see Whittier, who was staying at the "Squamscot House" (Blake's Hotel).

In November of 1860, B.B. French expressed his pleasure that Lincoln had become President-elect of these United States. "My political hopes so far are realized," he said.

His son, Francis, attended Phillips Exeter Academy while Amos Tuck was a Trustee there. There exists much communication between father Benjamin and his son, as the latter writes of his courtship of Tuck's daughter, Ellen, and the enjoyable visits at the Tuck home. When Frank married Ellen, the two fathers had agreed that the young couple would occupy the Tuck home. For a brief period of time, young French and Amos Tuck were partners in the latter's law firm.

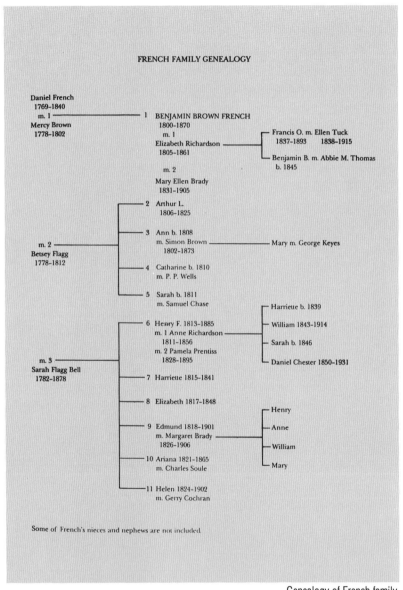

FRENCH FAMILY GENEALOGY

Daniel French
1769-1840
m. 1 ———————— 1 BENJAMIN BROWN FRENCH
Mercy Brown   1800-1870
1778-1802   m. 1
                       Elizabeth Richardson ———————— ⌐ Francis O. m. Ellen Tuck
                       1805-1861   1837-1893   1838-1915

                       m. 2   └ Benjamin B. m. Abbie M. Thomas
                                                        b. 1845
                       Mary Ellen Brady
                       1831-1905

                    2 Arthur L.
                       1806-1825

                    3 Ann b. 1808
m. 2   m. Simon Brown ———————— Mary m. George Keyes
Betsey Flagg   1802-1873
1778-1812
                    4 Catharine b. 1810
                       m. P. P. Wells

                    5 Sarah b. 1811
                       m. Samuel Chase

                                             ⌐ Harriette b. 1839

                    6 Henry F. 1813-1885   ─ William 1843-1914
                       m. 1 Anne Richardson ─
                       1811-1856   ─ Sarah b. 1846
                       m. 2 Pamela Prentiss
m. 3   1828-1895   └ Daniel Chester 1850-1931
Sarah Flagg Bell
1782-1878   7 Harriette 1815-1841

                    8 Elizabeth 1817-1848
                                             ⌐ Henry

                    9 Edmund 1818-1901   ─ Anne
                       m. Margaret Brady ────
                       1826-1906   ─ William

                   10 Ariana 1821-1865   └ Mary
                       m. Charles Soule

                   11 Helen 1824-1902
                       m. Gerry Cochran

Some of French's nieces and nephews are not included.

Genealogy of French family

SON, EDWARD TUCK, A TRIBUTE TO HIS FATHER

Upon graduation from Dartmouth in 1862, Edward Tuck had experienced some difficulty with his eyes, weakened from intensive study. Lincoln had been advised of his condition by Amos and when the young man recovered, he decided to take an examination for the consular service. Abraham Lincoln signed the parchment that made him an official in the United States diplomatic service at the age of twenty-two. Tuck's first financial training came to him in Paris, after his consular assignment was concluded, where he was offered a position with an American bank which brought him back to New York for a five-year apprenticeship. In 1871 he went back to France and made his home there. Edward Tuck became renowned in railroad, industrial, mining and banking enterprises, later becoming one of the principal American benefactors of latter-day France.

Eulogies appeared in newspapers worldwide, upon his death in Paris at the age of 96, in praise of his impressive success and great philanthropies, both in New Hampshire and in France.

The death notices included detailed biographical material, each of which referred to the influence of his father, Amos, in whose memory he had bequeathed such substantial gifts.

It was perhaps the death of his famous son, Edward, that brought to Amos some of his more significant and commemorative acknowledgments:

Boston Globe, **May 8, 1938:**

"His father, Amos Tuck, was among the men who founded the Republican party and it was he who chose the name that was given it. Edward Tuck honored his father's memory and established, at Dartmouth, the Amos Tuck School of Administration and Finance and, at Exeter, gave the Tuck High School building. The beautiful building in Concord of the New Hampshire Historical Society was an Edward Tuck gift and he helped the society in many other ways....To the town of Stratham he gave Stratham Hill...."

Boston Post, **May 1, 1938:**

"The great philanthropist's father, Amos Tuck, was one of the great figures of Exeter, a town whose roster contains more famous names than almost any other town in New England. The father was a devoted Abolitionist and worked untiringly for the freedom of slaves. He was for several years a member of Congress and was a delegate of the Philadelphia convention which founded the Republican party whose name, it is claimed, was given by Mr. Tuck. The elder was a life-long friend of Abraham Lincoln. The friendship began when the Prairie Statesman was unknown."

New York Herald Tribune, **May 1, 1938:**

Edward's "father was Amos Tuck, a rugged and fearless pioneer in New England politics whose ancestors landed from England somewhere near Plymouth Rock in 1636. Amos Tuck was organizer of the anti-slavery party in New Hampshire and served two (three) terms in Congress from 1847 to 1851. He was an intimate friend of Abraham Lincoln and was a member of the committee which informed the great liberator of his Presidential nomination. Amos Tuck attended the convention in Philadelphia at which the Republican party was founded and the name of the new group has since said to have been coined by the man from New Hampshire."

New York Times, **May 1, 1938:**

"His father, one of the organizers of the Anti-Slavery party in New Hampshire...has been described as one of the indirect means of the election of Abraham Lincoln as President. It is generally accepted that Lincoln's Cooper Union speech in the Spring of 1860 made him the Republican Presidential nominee. Lincoln delivered the address after he had started on his only visit to New England to see his son, Robert, who was a student at Phillips Exeter Academy. While in the New Hampshire school town, Lincoln was the guest of a former colleague in Congress, Amos Tuck, whose son, Edward was then a student at Dartmouth, a member of the class of 1862.

Amos became one of the staunchest supporters of Lincoln in the East, and the President expressed his gratitude in 1865 by appointing Edward Tuck as American Vice Consul in Paris under John Bigelow."

———◆———

Numerous Dartmouth publications provide stories on the Tucks, including the June 1937 issue of the *Dartmouth Alumni Magazine,* in an article "Mr. Tuck 75 Years after Graduation," by Francis Lane Childs. Amos Tuck is described as "an ardent leader in the anti-slavery movement, a member of Congress from New Hampshire for three terms and one of the founders of the national Republican party—the reform political group of its day."

Edward Tuck

The death in Paris of Edward Tuck deprived the state of New Hampshire of one of its most useful and most helpful sons. Born in Exeter and a graduate of Dartmouth College, Mr. Tuck had made his home is Paris for so many years that he was little more than a name to most New Hampshire people now living, but he did a great deal for his native state and only a few persons have any idea of the extent of his gifts.

His father, Amos Tuck, was among the men who founded the Republican party and it was he who chose the name that was given it. Edward Tuck honored his father's memory and established, at Dartmouth, the Amos Tuck School of Administration and Finance and, at Exeter, gave the Tuck High School building. The beautiful building in Concord of the New Hampshire Historical Society was an Edward Tuck gift and he helped that society in many other ways. A gift last year, of $2000 in cash, helped much in relieving a financial crisis that the society faced, because of reduced incomes due to the depression that started in 1929.

To the town of Stratham he gave Stratham Hill, the loftiest eminence in that section of the state, which has been converted into a public park and picnic ground.

There is another Tuck memorial that is not so greatly admired as are some of the others. On Star Island, in the Shoals group, stands a tall monument erected in honor of Rev. John Tuck, once a minister on the island, that is looked upon with disfavor by many of the group that now inhabits the island in Summer. Star is owned by the Isles of Shoals Association, made up of members of the Unitarian and Congregational religious groups, and while they admit the virtues of John Tuck, they look upon the obelisk that perpetuates his name as a bit out of place in such a setting. They feel that a monument not quite so tall and not quite so Egyptian in appearance would be more in keeping with the island surroundings.

John Tuck, an ancestor of Edward Tuck, was born at Hampton and was educated at Harvard. He was ordained on Star Island on July 26, 1732, and worked there as a minister until his death 41 years later. In those days there was a prosperous fishing settlement on Star Island and the offshore parish paid its ministers rather larger salaries than did many of those on the mainland.

Edward Tuck's death notice *The Boston Globe,* May 8, 1938

Amos Tuck's famous son, Edward *Exeter Historical Society*

IN WHICH STATE WAS THE REPUBLICAN PARTY BORN?

Many states claim the birthplace of the Republican party, but in *The Making Of The President 1964,* Theodore White records the three major contenders:

> **Some scholars still debate whether the first meeting of what became the Republican Party took place in Ripon, Wisconsin, in Jackson, Michigan—or in Exeter, New Hampshire.**

Although the early stirrings of the Republican party occurred prior to the mid-1850s, it appears that little note was taken of the significance of its origin until more than two decades later. In 1874, Henry Wilson, in his *Rise and Fall of Slave Power in America,* was the first recognized historian to chronicle the beginning of the party, which came to be known as the Republican party of Lincoln.

Wilson's version of history concluded that, "One of the earliest, if not the earliest, of the movements that contemplated definite action in the formation of a new party, was made in Ripon, Fond du Lac County, Wisconsin, in the early months of 1854."

In addition to Wilson's crediting Ripon as one of the early birthplaces of the Republican Party, he honored Jackson for its share of the glory: "Whatever suggestions others may have made, or whatever actions may have been taken elsewhere, to Michigan belongs the honor of being the first state to form and christen the Republican party."

While Henry Wilson did not mention Tuck's 1853 meeting at Blake's Hotel, it is significant that the historian recognized Amos' foresight in having established a new political party in 1845 and the introduction of its newspaper to censure slavery. It had been Tuck's idea to engage his friend, George Fogg, to publish the paper, known as the Independent Democrat.

The combination of that meeting and the resultant newspaper was the first organized initiative advocating abolition.

Wilson commented:

> **Under the lead of Amos Tuck,** who had already taken an active part in giving expression and direction to the popular disfavor against such high handed tyranny (slavery), they at once prepared for action....Stimulated by their success, and continuing the struggle with increased determination and vigor, they established at the State capital the "Independent Democrat," under the editorial control of George G. Fogg. It was conducted with signal ability and tact, rendered essential service, and contributed largely to the triumph of **this first successful revolt against the iron depostism of the Slave Power.**

Though born in New Hampshire, Wilson moved to Massachusetts where he began his political career by serving in the Bay State legislature in 1840. Later, he was elected Congressman, then Senator from Massachusetts. In 1873, he served as Vice President under Ulysses S. Grant.

Wilson was never involved in the Free Soil or Republican movements in New Hampshire and presumably had no knowledge of the Exeter meeting of 1853.

In *Rise and Fall,* Wilson made one reference to New Hampshire: "Strenuous efforts were made to combine the Free Soilers, Whigs, and the Anti-Nebraska Democrats in some common action; and these efforts were so far successful as to prevent the election of a Democrat, although they failed to elect their candidate. It was, however, the beginning of a process by the operation of which the majority of **the state (New Hampshire) became Republican in fact and name,** and sent John P. Hale to the Senate in 1855 to fill Mr. Atherton's term and James Bell for the full term." The process to which Wilson referred had begun in 1844.

Wilson's conclusions somehow established him as an authority on the founding of the party, on whose research many historians later relied.

What instigated Wilson's research in the party's origin, and why no one appears to have previously treated the subject seriously, remains a mystery. Perhaps the Civil War, from 1861–65, dominated the historical focus, or there may have been some uncertainty as to the party's potential strength and longevity.

We know that Wilson was described by historian George H. Mayer as a chameleon, and that he had admitted to John L. Hayes his omission of an important chapter of New Hampshire history in his 1874 chronicle. Still, Wilson's book had an impact, which gave rise to claims from other states and eventually, to a myriad of interpretations from various historians.

In 1884, ten years later, historian Frank A. Flower repeated Wilson's views in his *History of the Republican Party*. Flower described his book as "a more authentic and detailed account of the early organization, struggles and disciples of the Republican party than has hitherto been published in any form whatsoever." The preface included sketches of "Republican State movements in 1854" thereby acknowledging by omission that he had not considered what occurred in 1853.

A gap appears to exist in the Party's history between 1853 and 1874, when Wilson studied the Free Soilers, and from 1874 to 1884, when Flower wrote his history of the Party. Both authors relied on the clamor made by the principal, and ruggedly persistent claimant Alvan Bovay. In fact, most of the later historians began their research in 1854, rather than in 1853, the same year Wilson and Flower had overlooked.

A similar historical gap occurred from 1927 to 1956, according to Malcolm Moos who wrote that "several factors prompted the decision to write this book *(The Republicans, A History of Their Party)*. An obvious one was that no Republican party history had appeared for almost thirty years." To his credit and because A. J. Turner had mentioned it in his *Genesis of the Republican Party,* published in 1898, Moos did make reference to the Exeter meeting of 1853.

Even contemporary historian George Mayer neglected to go back far enough when he wrote in 1964, "Although few people recognized it at the time, the initial round of protest meetings in February and March (1854) was the beginning of the Republican party."

THE BIRTH—AS VIEWED BY
THE REPUBLICAN PARTY

In 1956, the Republican National Committee published a pamphlet, *The History of the Republican Party 1854–1956*, which stated:

> **The Republican Party was born in 1854. There is no dispute as to the year of its formal organization, although debate still goes on as to the exact birthplace. Both Ripon, Wisconsin, and Jackson, Michigan, claim the honor.**

After reviewing material sent to them from Hugh Gregg's book, *A Tall State Revisited—A Republican Perspective*, the Republican National Committee amended its statement on the origin of the Republican Party. In its update of August 1994, *Even More In '94—A Handbook for Republican Involvement*, published by the RNC, the authors added a new admission:

> **The location of the first meeting has been disputed....Some evidence indicates an earlier meeting was held in Exeter, New Hampshire.**

In substantiation of Exeter's peremptory claim as the indisputable birthplace of the Republican Party and Amos Tuck's role in its formation, there follows an analysis of Ripon and Jackson's claims as compared to Exeter.

A Brief History
of the
Republican Party

1956 Rendition

"The Republican Party was born in 1854. There is no dispute as to the year of its formal organization, although debate still goes on as to the exact birthplace. Both Ripon, Wisconsin, and Jackson, Michigan, claim the honor."

1993 Rendition

"The first stirrings of the Republican Party came in February, 1854, when Whig Party defectors met privately in Crawfordsville, Iowa, to call for the creation of a new political party. The first public meeting was held one month later at a small church in Ripon, Wisconsin, when Alan Bovay rallied anti-slavery forces and adopted resolutions opposing the Kansas-Nebraska Act."

1994 Rendition

"Evidence indicates there were several groups across the country that met to discuss the formation of a new party. Thus, the location of the first meeting has been disputed. It is known that Whig Party defectors met privately in Crawfordsville, Iowa, to call for the creation of a new political party. **Some evidence indicates an earlier meeting was held in Exeter, New Hampshire.** The first public meeting was held in March of 1854 <u>at a small church</u> in Ripon, Wisconsin, when Alan Bovay rallied anti-slavery ..."

A Brief History of the Republican Party

RIPON, WISCONSIN
(1995 POPULATION 7,200)

It was not until May 29, 1848, that Wisconsin was admitted to the union as the thirtieth state (in contrast to New Hampshire which had adopted its Constitution seventy-two years earlier). In 1849 the village of Ripon, formerly called "Ceresco," was organized (Exeter had been colonized over two centuries earlier).

Ripon was named by a former Territorial Governor after his family's ancestral home in England, a cathedral city located in Yorkshire. Situated in a fertile agricultural area, today its two major industries are Speed Queen, manufacturers of washers and dryers, and Ripon Foods, one of the nation's largest producers of cookies.

The effective, long-term promotion of Ripon, Wisconsin, as the birthplace of the GOP led, over the years, to the general assumption that it was properly designated. The city's uncontested claim caused many Republicans, unfamiliar with Amos Tuck or Exeter, to accept Ripon as the original home of the party. The legend is based on the chronological fact that the Ripon meetings had occurred prior to the one at Jackson.

Ripon's claim has been reinforced by the aggressive commercialization of the Ripon community, where one of its early "Republican" meeting sites has become the town's focal point as a tourist attraction. The Ripon Chamber of Commerce has even alleged that in 1896 the Republican National Convention meeting in St. Louis accepted Ripon's claim "without qualification."

However, neither the official minutes of that Convention nor records in the Library of Congress discloses any such certifica-tion, nor has the RNC otherwise anointed Ripon as the solitary birthplace of the Republican party.

Wisconsin newspapers have also been protective of Ripon's claim and have been substantially helpful in promoting it.

Ripon's place in Republican Party history resulted from the entrepreneurship of the activist, Alvan E. Bovay.

Welcome to Ripon, Wisconsin *Cay Gregg*

Oshkosh
Northwestern

THURSDAY MORNING, OCTOBER 14, 1993 | PUBLISHED IN OSHKOSH, WIS. | 80 PAGES/50 cents

Ripon claim challenged

N.H. town says it is true GOP birthplace

Exeter's claim

According to Former Gov. Hugh Gregg, Exeter's claim to the title include:

▶ **DOCUMENTATION BY** Congressmen Amos Tuck about the Exeter meeting and the purpose for it being called. It consisted of 14 state-wide politicians from several parties, all with the same concern about slavery. John P. Hale, a U.S. Senator from New Hampshire, also helped organize the meeting and attended, Gregg said.

▶ **HORACE GREELEY,** publisher of the New York Times, published the meeting's purpose in his newspaper shortly after, indicating the name Republican was given.

▶ **A PLAQUE** was placed in 1929 on Exeter's Gorham Hall, the place of the 1853 meeting. It described what happened there.

▶ **THE DOCUMENTATION** about the meeting has been confirmed by a Ph.D. at the State Archives, New Hampshire's Secretary of State, scholars at the New Hampshire State Historical Society and the Exeter historian, Gregg said.

Ripon's claim

Ripon claims to be the Republican birthplace as of March 20, 1854, in the Little White Schoolhouse. A meeting was held to form a new party, and the name Republican was given. There were 54 citizens who attended, three of whom were women. Ripon has three undisputable claims for being the Republican party birthplace, Chamber Executive Director Carolyn Seawell said. They are:

▶ **THE 1896** Republican National Convention in St. Louis officially designated Ripon the birthplace.

▶ **THE LITTLE** White Schoolhouse, which was the meeting place, is on the National Register of Historic Places.

▶ **THE ENCYCLOPEDIA** Britannica designates Ripon as the birthplace.

▶ **"WE ALSO** have local information about the meeting that Alan Bovay called and his discussion with Horace Greeley in 1852," Seawell said.

Oshkosh Northwestern, October 14, 1993

ALVAN EARLE BOVAY

Locally pronounced "Bovee", the prime advocate of Ripon's claim was born July 12, 1818 (eight years after Amos Tuck) in Adams, New York. A graduate of Norwich University in Vermont, he taught at academies in Pennsylvania and New York. In 1846, he was married and admitted to the New York bar (eleven years after Tuck's admission in New Hampshire).

He practiced law in New York City where, as a Whig, he became involved in the "National Reform Association," a group dedicated to the rights of the individual in public lands and against rental procedures in the East. At one time he edited a publication entitled Young America whose motto was "Vote Yourself A Farm."

Like Amos Tuck, Bovay supported the Homestead Law, which encouraged emigrants to move into the western territories. The settlers were given land to occupy and work for several years, after which they made install-ment repayments to the government. The law was eventually enacted, under Republican sponsorship, in 1862.

During the period when living in New York, mid-to-late 1840s, Bovay became acquainted with Horace Greeley, editor of the New York Tribune, the country's most influential newspaper of the time. Greeley had been born in Amherst and had lived in Londonderry, both New Hampshire towns within a few miles of Exeter. He frequently returned from New York to visit his native state.

Alvan E. Bovay *Framk A. Flower*

BOVAY MOVES WEST

In late 1850 Bovay left New York for the little Wisconsin prairie village. As related by historian Malcolm Moos, "Bovay arrived in Ripon on October 5, 1850, looking for a home after tramping seventy-five miles from Milwaukee, where he had left his family." The community's population was 350. (At that time Exeter had 3,329 residents).

Upon arrival, Bovay was befriended by and moved in with Captain David P. Mapes, a developer and promoter busily engaged in attracting settlers to the fledgling community. Bovay soon discovered that dealing in real estate was far more lucrative than practicing law, and joined Mapes in "selling" the town. It is reported, by Ripon College Professor A. F. Gilman, that he became "the promoter of Bovay's Addition, a real estate venture that substantially enlarged the village's boundaries."

Mapes was a dedicated Democrat. The two worked well together, as Mapes explained: "Our political paths have not always run in the same direction, but in that we have found our account, as changes in party have frequently occurred; when his party (Bovay's) was in power he would go to court for favors, and when my side was up I would go, and we were both lucky in carrying our points for Ripon."

The enterprising Governing District appropriated $300 to build a school, hoping to encourage the formation of a college in Ripon. Bovay earned the gratitude of the townspeople by donating a site to the District upon which a white school house was constructed. At one time the one-room clapboard structure actually became part of the Ripon College campus. The building also served as a headquarters for community activities.

Much later, in 1884, Captain Mapes recalled how "the tallow candle kept its light in the little white school house…long after midnight" when Bovay used to work there "making a bit of history."

A politically-active Whig Alan Bovay attended that party's convention of 1852 where, at Lovejoy's Hotel in New York City, he met once again with Horace Greeley. But it is significant to note that he did not record that encounter until he wrote a letter to author Frank A. Flower over thirty years later, wherein he recalled having suggested to Greeley that a new party, named Republican, should be formed. He reported that Greeley, a loyal Whig, did not agree, because he thought the Whig party was still strong.

Greeley's political instinct had been wrong. The Whig presidential nominee, Winfield Scott, was defeated by New Hampshire's Franklin Pierce. Ironically, another New Hampshire player had his own aspirations. Daniel Webster had, himself, aspired to be the Whig nominee at the 1852 convention.

On February 28, 1854 (or the correct date may have been March 1, 1854) a town meeting was called by Bovay and others at the Congregational Church in Ripon to remonstrate against the Nebraska Act, then before the Congress, which would have extended slavery. This was over four months after the second Exeter meeting and **nine years after the slavery issue had first been raised at the earlier Exeter meeting.**

(Note: The Nebraska Act, also known as the Kansas-Nebraska Bill, would have repealed the Missouri Compromise of 1820 and the Compromise of 1850 which had prohibited slavery in the Northwest Territory. In lieu thereof the Act provided that the inhabitants of that region could decide for themselves if they wished to permit slavery until the area became states of the union.)

By March 20, 1854, the U. S. Senate had passed the Act and it was being considered in the House of Representatives. Acting quickly, Bovay and his friends called a second town meeting, this time at the little white school house of District No. 2, for more definitive reaction to the bill.

(Note: In an 1899 interview published in the *Commonwealth* of November 8th, Bovay said there was a third meeting, the first two held in the church, and that fifty-four citizens had attended the second meeting in the church. He was then 81 years old and in ill health, thus possibly confused in both the substance and sequence of his recollections.)

Schoolhouse in which Bovay held his first Republican meeting *Frank A. Flower*

Curiously enough, Frank Flower included on page 149 of his book a photo of the school house with the cut line: "School House in which Bovay held his first Republican meeting."

In one of his interviews in the mid-1880s Bovay recalled that the objective of the school house meeting had been to take the necessary steps to form a new party. Yet, the call of the meeting published in the *Ripon Herald* on March 15th made no such reference; rather, the stated purpose was to organize against the Nebraska Act. Years later Bovay remembered that fifty-four local citizens had attended, who "dissolved their local committees and chose five men to serve as the committee for the new party."

Bovay told Samuel Pedrick, his biographer, "The name (Republican) was well settled in my mind as the organization (for the new party), and I took what seemed to me the most effectual course to secure its general adoption…that I was advocating this name for the great party which I saw looming in the near future above the horizon, as far back as the autumn of 1852…It was not until June 1854, that the name Republican was formally adopted, and that was by the state convention of Michigan."

In his 1874 interview with Wilson, Bovay further spelled out his dream: "The adoption of the name was as much inevitable to success as was the nomination of Abraham Lincoln in 1860."

BOVAY CEASES POLITICAL ACTIVITY

Except for the two Ripon meetings motivated by Alan Bovay there is no record that he organized subsequent rallies to form a new party. In July of 1854 he attended and was appointed Secretary of the Wisconsin State Convention. But, according to

Ripon historian, George Miller, he was otherwise ignored by the Wisconsin Republican Party, nor is there any evidence that he ever participated in its affairs or undertook any further political activity.

Apparently after 1854 Bovay continued practicing law and dabbling in real estate, as shown in an ad that appeared in the May 6, 1884 issue of the *Ripon Herald:*

ALVAN E. BOVAY

Attorney and Counsellor at Law, and Notary
Public Ripon, Fond du Lac County, Wisconsin.
Oaths administered, deeds and mortgages drawn,
acknowledgements taken, etc. on reasonable terms.
Also, offers for sale 100 lots of ground with title
perfect in Ripon, Ceresco, and Bovay's addition.

His biographer, Samuel Pedrick, wrote that during the last thirty years of his life, while still living in Ripon, "Mr. Bovay seems to have been somewhat quiet politically, if we can judge by his comments in the Ripon newspapers."

This contrasts dramatically with the life of Amos Tuck who, both before and after the Exeter meetings, was actively arranging and participating in "Indignation Meetings" all over the State of New Hampshire. [Editor's Note: See pages 20-23.]

"REPUBLICAN" NAME NOT ADOPTED AT RIPON

The First Meeting

One of the resolutions that had been unanimously passed at the Ripon church meeting was:

Resolved: That the passage of this bill (if it should pass) will be to call to arms of a great Northern party, such as the country has not hitherto seen, composed of Whigs, Democrats and Free-Soilers; every man with a heart in him united under the single banner cry of "Repeal! Repeal!"

Henry Wilson interpreted the resolution to mean that if the Nebraska Act should become law, then they would "throw old party organizations to the winds, and organize a new party on the sole issue of the non-extension of slavery."

Francis Curtis, another respected historian, published *The Republican Party* in 1904. He had talked with Bovay, as had Wilson and Flower. Curtis carried his analysis of the meeting one step further, stating that if the Bill passed, a new party should be organized "to be called Republican, formed on the sole issue of opposition to slavery extension."

There is, however, no record anywhere that the word "Republican" was used in relation to the meeting at the church.

The Second Meeting

In an article published in the *Commonwealth* on September 26, 1900, Bovay is quoted on the school house meeting:

I made a speech laying out all the plans. 'I can't tell you what the name of our new party should be, but I can tell you what it ought to be.' And then I proposed the name 'Republican.' It was well received....

We formed a permanent organization, putting upon our committee of five representatives of all the factions. This was the first meeting of the Republican party of today.

The very next day I wrote Mr. Greeley all about it…and said, 'I want you to propose the new name Republican and a new party organization….'

The answer came back: 'You do it yourself. You know I'll publish anything you write.

I answered: 'The idea of a correspondent will have no weight. You must do it editorially.

But he didn't do it for some time though eventually the editorial columns carried the suggestion, tersely, pungently, effectively, so that it was at once adopted all over the country.

Note: It was not until June of 1854 that Greeley named the party "Republican" in the *Tribune*.

Although the local *Ripon Herald* gave a full account of the actions taken at the first meeting in the church, no record was published of what took place at this second meeting. Nor have historians discovered any contemporaneous record of what happened at the second meeting. Bovay however, in a letter written over three decades later, recounted, "We went into the little meeting Whigs, Free Soilers, and Democrats. We came out Republicans and…were the first Republicans in the Union."

Wilson disagrees:

> **Bovay, though stating his belief that the party should and probably would take the name of 'Republican,' advised against such a christening at that time and by that small body of local men.**

Bovay's reaction as stated to Pedrick, his biographer, was "Wilson's history is very brief, but it is substantially correct."

Bovay himself confirmed Wilson's analysis by a further statement in the *Commonwealth* interview wherein Bovay recalled: "At this meeting (in the school house) I offered the name 'Republican' for the new party, but did not consider it proper to use the name until the party had assumed more of a national character."

Thus, the name "Republican" was not adopted at either of the Ripon meetings.

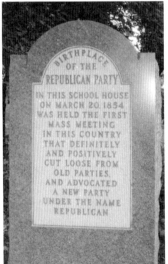

Historic marker at
Ripon school house
Cay Gregg

Historic marker on
Ripon school house
Cay Gregg

Historians Comment

Francis Curtis explained that during the time of the anti-Nebraska insurgencies there were "thousands of local and minor gatherings, which were for every purpose Republican, and which were afterwards looked upon by the participants as Republican gatherings. At the same time the use of the word Republican was the exception rather than the rule."

Or, as Wilson commented with reference to the school house meeting: "Whether there was or was not in this general uprising any local action which antedated it, few will question Bovay when he said: 'The actors in this remote little eddy of politics thought at the time they were making a bit of history by that solitary tallow candle in the little white school-house on the prairie; and whether ever recognized and published or not, they think so still.'"

Note: *Newsweek's Travel Guide to the United States* lists Ripon as the birthplace of the Republican Party, stating that while a new party was formed at the school house in 1854, it was not formally named until two years later.

CONTRAST OF RIPON MEETINGS TO EXETER'S

Both meetings called by Bovay were attended by friends and residents of the town. There were no statewide leaders in attendance. Bovay himself did not seek political office until 1858, when he served two one-year terms in the Wisconsin legislature.

In contrast the Exeter meeting consisted of leaders from the various splinter political parties who represented widespread geographical areas of New Hampshire.

New Hampshire historian Elwin L. Page aptly observed: **"Tuck had four groups to organize, and he had to win a state, not a small town and neighbors."**

The Bovays Correspond with Greeley

Bovay was still alive at the time of Flower's writing in 1884, and correspondence between them is reproduced in Flower's book. Bovay, his wife, Captain Mapes and another friend, in letters to Flower, meticulously recalled what they say had transpired three decades earlier. Thus, the story of what occurred at Ripon, as hereinbefore and hereinafter related, was re-created by Bovay, long after the experience.

Bovay also recounted to Flower that he had written letters to Horace Greeley on February 26th and June 12th, 1854, again urging him to name a new party, Republican. On June 16th, 1854, Greeley's editorial in the *New York Daily Tribune* entitled "Party Names and Public Duty" (reprinted in the *Weekly Tribune* on June 24th) did endorse the name Republican but credited no one for having suggested it.

Appropriately it was the same name Thomas Jefferson had used in 1801 and later adopted by Henry Clay in 1831 as the National Republican party.

But Greeley Made No Mention of Bovay or the Ripon Meetings

Bovay's wife was so distressed at what she considered a slight to her husband that she wrote to Frank A. Flower on March 2, 1884: "I felt aggrieved that Greeley, after the name (Republican) was accepted and grew famous and strong, never so much as alluded to whence the suggestion came. He had the magnanimity never to claim it for himself. Had he done so, I should have made a fuss."

She did not know Dr. Batchelder and Amos Tuck had previously advised Greeley of the use of the name Republican at the Exeter meeting which had occurred earlier in 1853.

Others Comment on the Ripon Meetings

Greeley's June editorials of 1854 suggesting the name 'Republican' were preceded by the 1853 comments of editor Joseph Medill writing in a Cleveland newspaper, *Daily Forest City.* Journalist Andrew Turner said Medill, who had been in correspondence with both Greeley and John P. Hale, "wrote a series of articles advocating the selection of the name 'Republican' for the new party, which he proposed should replace the Whig party."

Even noted historian Francis Curtis, who supported Ripon's claim as the party's birthplace, admitted in *The Republican Party:*

It is not claimed here that Bovay is the creator of the Republican party. The spirit was active in 1854, in every village and city in the free states, which would have created the party even if Bovay and Greeley had never been born.

In New Hampshire, the Party's development enjoyed the unrelenting guidance of one steady hand. It was Amos Tuck who masterminded it from those early days of protest, to the election of his friend, Abraham Lincoln, to the presidency. Obviously Curtis had no knowledge that New Hampshire had already planted the seed at Exeter in 1845 and plucked the bloom in 1853!

Said Andrew Wallace Crandall, in *The Early History of the Republican Party 1854-56,* "The meeting at Ripon, WI, February 28, fathered by Alvan E. Bovay, has a very respectable support in its claim to first place, **although it is not universally accepted.**" He admitted that New Hampshire gave the Republican Party its first great boost with its "virtual defeat" of Democratic presidential candidate Pierce in his home state.

Dr. William H. Mandrey, in "How the Republican Party Got Its Name," *New Hampshire Profiles,* July-August 1972, goes so far as to suggest, "When the sponsors of a new party met at Ripon, Wisconsin, in March 1854 they unanimously adopted Tuck's suggestion that they be known as the Republican Party."

THE LITTLE WHITE SCHOOL HOUSE

Historic marker at
school house site
Cay Gregg

Similar photos have been widely dispersed, such as a cherry framed copy priced at $59.95 (plus $7.05 shipping) and offered by *SkyMall* magazine (summer 94) which is distributed free to 800,000 airline passengers on a daily basis.

Eventually the student population outgrew the old school house, built in 1853, and Ripon college built a larger brick structure. Thus in 1860, the clapboard building was altered and occupied as a residence for more than thirty years. It has been moved several times and was converted to a college museum in 1908. In l951, it was given to the Foundation for American Principles and Traditions, a local group of philanthropic citizens dedicated to its preservation, who raised the funds for its maintenance. Today the national tourist attraction is located on Blackburn Street (Hwy. 23).

In l973 the school house was listed in the *National Register of Historic Places*. In 1974 it was declared a National Historic Landmark, currently identified by four historic markers. A portable replica of the building is towed behind an automobile for parades and to exhibits.

"Church in which Bovay named the Republican Party." — *Frank Flower*

Portable replica of the school house *Cay Gregg*

Again, curiously, Frank Flower included on page 157 of his book a photo of the church with the cut line: "in which Bovay named the Republican Party."

Because it is well preserved, quaint, and was largely Bovay's creation, it is no surprise he sought to fix the party's birthplace there, rather than at the Ripon Congregational Church, which would appear to have had the stronger claim. It was in the church where the first gathering was held and the actions taken were published. Though the original church was replaced several years ago, it was still there in 1884 when Bovay was refreshing his recollections of what had occurred in 1854.

The Ripon Chamber of Commerce, which administers the school house as the city's major historic site, estimates that it hosts 10,000 visitors annually. The interior has been restructured as the original classroom with interesting artifacts that include a teacher's desk alleged to have been used by Bovay. A wide assortment of trinkets and souvenirs, from pencils and bookmarks to T-shirts, and even a cookbook with a recipe for "Elephant Stew," are promoted for sale.

ELEPHANT STEW

1 med. size elephant	16 lb. carrots, diced
26 lbs. onion, sliced	2 large rabbits

Cut elephant into bite size pieces. This should take about 6 weeks. Add enough brown gravy to cover. Add vegetables. Cook on Weber grill for about 5 weeks at 350°. This will feed 4,000 people. If more people are expected, add 2 rabbits, but do this only if necessary, as most people do not like to find a "hare" in their stew.

—From *The Birthplace of the Republican Party* cookbook, Clark Kaufmann and Chris Schultz, Ripon, Wisconsin.

On the inside wall of the school house is posted a framed list of other sites which had made claim to being the birthplace of the Republican party. Nine such locations are identified, yet, up to 1995, Exeter had not been included. This is a further indication that the boosters of Ripon didn't know of the early action taken in New Hampshire.

Interior of the school house *Cay Gregg*

The school house steps have been used as a backdrop for such events as when Secretary of War, Patrick J. Hurley, launched President Herbert Hoover's re-election campaign there in 1932. Great pride is taken in the site's endorsement by the *Encyclopedia Britannica*.

Of more questionable value is their boast that Democrat Ted Kennedy had been a visitor in his youth. It is reported that when William Jennings Bryant toured the school house he remarked that he wasn't particularly interested in where the Republican party was born, but he'd have a keen interest in seeing where it was buried.

In 1970, New Hampshire Legislative Historian, Leon W. Anderson, investigating the Ripon claim, received a response from the President of the Ripon Republican Club. It stated, "We had not previously learned (prior to Anderson's inquiry) of the Exeter meeting sponsored by Amos Tuck more than four months before the meeting in Ripon called by Alvan E. Bovay." Thus, it's unlikely that even twenty five years ago Ripon Republican activists were cognizant of the action previously taken in New Hampshire.

The Ripon Club President also raised a tantalizing theory when he wrote, "It would be interesting to know if Bovay was acquainted with Tuck or present at the dinner meeting in Exeter." He wasn't. **On the other hand, he may well have been influenced by John P. Hale, as early as the fall of 1852!**

John P. Hale
NH Historical Society

NEW HAMPSHIRE'S JOHN P. HALE INSPIRES WISCONSIN

Long before Wisconsin's 1854 convention, John P. Hale, a Free-Soiler from New Hampshire, had already served in the Senate since 1847, and was nationally recognized as the first anti-slavery member of that body. In that year he had also been nominated for President by the Liberty/Free Soil Party, but declined after Martin Van Buren was nominated by the Democrats in 1848.

In 1852, he ran as the Liberty/Free-Soil Party nominee for President against victorious New Hampshire Democrat, Franklin Pierce. Nonetheless Hale was very much in demand for the stirring speeches he was giving throughout the country against slavery and the annexation of states that wished to extend it.

The *Milwaukee Sentinel* of October 2, 1852, reported:

> Senator Hale—The Free Democrat announces that Mr. Hale, the Free Soil Candidate for the presidency, will be in this state week after next and spend three days here. Mr. Hale is a capital speaker and will be listened to with interest and pleasure even by those who do not share his practical opinions.

For four days, from October 11th through the 14th, Hale delivered a series of speeches in a number of Wisconsin communities where he attracted audiences of 4,000-5,000 at some stops. Driven from Waukesha to Milwaukee, the horses were attired with HALE signs on their heads—perhaps a precursor of today's bumper stickers.

On October l3th the *Milwaukee Sentinel* noted: "Mr. Hale is a man of great talent, and high character, one of the best speakers in the Union."

On the following day the paper compared him to Stephen Douglas saying:

> "No man, whatever may be his political views, can listen to Mr. Hale without pleasure and profit. Mr. Douglas, on the contrary, disgusts both friends and opponents. The one appeals to the reason, the conscience and the hearts of his auditors; the other to their passions and prejudices…he (Douglas) does not approach John P. Hale in power, eloquence, or effect."

The Hale visit was given extensive publicity and attracted mammoth crowds. Considering that two years earlier Bovay had walked from Milwaukee to Ripon, it is quite possible he might have attended any one of the meetings addressed by Hale in Wisconsin or even a speech Hale delivered in Milwaukee. Perhaps it was Hale's rhetoric that inspired Bovay to call the Ripon meetings fifteen months later.

On July 13, 1854, Wisconsin held a state convention, adopted the name Republican and took pride in sending a Free-Soiler (not a Republican, though he subsequently became one), Charles Durkee, to the U.S. Senate. The Free-Soil party had taken a strong stand against slavery nationwide, and was a harbinger of the Republican Party.

HALE'S ROLE IN THE FOUNDING

Hale and Amos Tuck had led both the 1845 and 1853 meetings at Exeter. In 1858, Hale was re-elected to the Senate as a Republican.

Colonel Daniel Hall, State Chairman of the Republican Committee, in his "Occasional Addresses" delivered at Dover and Concord in October 1892, gave much credit to John P. Hale for pioneering the great Free-soil movement that finally overthrew slavery in the United States, "New Hampshire was the first battlefield of the new crusade, and John P. Hale commanded the vanguard."

Hall continued:

> The Hon. Amos Tuck, one of the earliest, ablest, and most faithful of the followers of Mr. Hale, at Downer Landing in 1878, met the claim of Massachusetts that the Republican party was founded there in 1848, **by showing that the party was anticipated in every one of its ideas by the Hale party in New Hampshire in 1845,** and that John P. Hale won his election as the first anti-slavery senator, and sat in that body, alone, as such, for two years before a friendly senator came to join him, and two years before the date which Massachusetts claims for her patent.
>
> This claim for New Hampshire and for Mr. Hale is impregnable. Therefore I say that no man can precede Mr. Hale as the founder of the Republican party, and all that is implied thereby: and that whatever of merit may attach to such a sponsorship—and I know full well that many still regard it as a cause for condemnation rather than praise—that whatever of glory or shame there be in it, belongs to him more than to any other man.

(Note: It was thanks to the initiative and infallible support of his close friend Amos Tuck that Hale ran for the Senate in 1847.)

In a letter from Tuck to George G. Fogg, dated March 14, 1876, Tuck wrote,

> when Hale had been elected to the Senate, he told me, at Dover, in the Fall of 1846, on a walk to Garrison Hill, …that he had been saved by the action at Exeter, and never was more surprised in his life, than when, at New Bedford, he learnt that Woodbury was defeated.

Tuck continued,

> I shall endeavor to do scrupulous justice to Mr. Hale, but I cannot, of course, as I proceed, endorse the delusion, and attempts to impress it into history, that he originated or carried on the organization in New Hampshire, which through many years fought the good fight and kept the faith in the Granite State. He did the conspicuous, creditably and satisfactorily, and we gave him the palm and the laurels….We,—that is, you and I, and others—fought out the Kansas issue, till we got the control again in New Hampshire, and then Mr. Hale came back again, ignored but did not deny his removal to New York, and again we put upon his brow the honors achieved for him, not by him.
>
> We did it without grudging, for we were busy in our affairs, not being politicians….We both know the past, and while I intend to be very scrupulous, and all the more, for your friendly admonition, I must take care, as I proceed, not to belie history, nor strain it, as it has been in the past, for the purpose of confirming erroneous impression.

It appears that at this point in his life, Tuck had come to recognize that the claim to the founding of the Party was becoming an issue.

TUCK KNEW LINCOLN…
BOVAY NEVER MET HIM

During the Republican campaigns of 1856 and 1860 Bovay never met Lincoln. However, in a letter to Greeley dated June 17, 1860, he gave Greeley credit for engineering Lincoln's presidential nomination at the Chicago convention and congratulated him for it.

Although Lincoln had never visited Ripon, as he had Exeter, a beautiful statue of a "young" Lincoln stands on the grounds of Ripon College. It was presented to the college by the sculptor, Clarence Addison Shaler, an 1881 graduate.

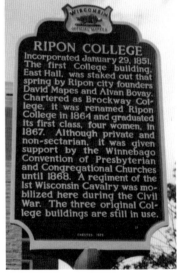

Left, Lincoln statue at Ripon College
Above, Ripon College marker
Photos by Cay Cregg

In 1847, Amos Tuck of New Hampshire, Abraham Lincoln of Illinois and New York's Horace Greeley had been elected to the 30th United States Congress. Greeley had filled a vacancy, served three months and was not renominated. After one term, Lincoln returned to Illinois and the practice of law. Tuck was re-elected to both the 31st and 32nd Congresses.

Said Amos Tuck, "In the fourth seat at my left sat a new member from Illinois, the only Whig from that State, a tall, awkward, genial 'good fellow,' the future President of the United States, Abraham Lincoln…." Lincoln, a celebrated tale-teller himself, "would come over to his seat (Tuck's), saying, 'Come, Tuck, tell me some New England stories' which he was sure of hearing well told." (Rev. George E. Street)

According to Tuck's autobiography, the friendship formed between Mr. Lincoln and Tuck in that Congress continued throughout his life.

The Name "Republican" Was Often Used

Tuck, Lincoln and Greeley had become close friends. Greeley even suggested Tuck as one of two most deserving to be United States Senator from New Hampshire. It was during the same period that Tuck was fervently promoting the principles he had espoused at the meeting in the First Congregational Church in Exeter on February 22, 1845.

Thus, it is logical that Tuck and Greeley, when serving together in Congress in 1848, frequently discussed the identification of a new party. Tuck had already asserted his own independence and concern for the vital issues of the day by leaving the Democrats in 1845. From that date until he was elected to Congress in 1847, the overriding objective of his New Hampshire election campaign was to press the need for a realignment of party structures.

We remember that Tuck's friends Ichabod Bartlett, William Plumer, Jr., and William H.Y. Hackett had played prominent roles at the 1828 meeting in Concord, New Hampshire, when they had chosen electors for the "National Republican Ticket."

This same trio attended the October 12, 1853, meeting at Blake's Hotel in Exeter when the name Republican was again chosen for the new party. Thus, the name Republican was familiar to and favored by Tuck long before he went to Congress.

The fundamental Republican principles espoused by Tuck eventually became the basis of the Republican national platforms. George Fogg served on the platform committee at the 1856 convention and Tuck served in the same capacity in 1860.

It was Amos Tuck's vigorous leadership that succeeded in bringing together the many and varied dissident political factions that existed, when New Hampshire was the most Democratic state in the country. In 1852 the state had elected a Democratic governor, Noah Martin, a Democratic legislature, and Democrat Franklin Pierce as President — all of whom had been elected by large majorities. Democratic party control of the state had been absolute since 1829.

Partisan political activities in the Granite State were even noted in the *Ripon Herald* of March 15, 1854: "The Democrats of New Hampshire have elected their Governor and a majority of the legislature though by a decreased vote." [Note: Even in the 1850s New Hampshire was first-in-the-nation.]

JACKSON, MICHIGAN
(1995 POPULATION 37,400)

As anti-slavery sentiment fermented all over the country, other states took new political direction.

On July 6, 1854, Michigan held a statewide convention in Jackson. The call for the meeting was made to those who were "ready to sink all other political differences and unite to oppose the extension of slavery." The crowd was so large it had to be held outdoors "in a beautiful oak grove located between the village and the county race track."

A full slate of Republican candidates was nominated which consisted of three Free-soilers, five Whigs, and two anti-Nebraska Democrats who had voted for Franklin Pierce in 1852. Because the participants in this convention were representative of a wider geographical area and passed formal resolutions, a few historians view Jackson as a more appropriate birthplace of the party than Ripon. James Ford Rhodes wrote in his *History of the United States Compromise of 1850,* "This differed from other meetings held throughout the North in that the organization of a new party on the slavery issue was recommended, and the name suggested for it was 'Republican'."

At the Jackson Convention it was: "Resolved, that in view of the necessity of battling for the first principles of Republican government, and against the schemes of aristoc-racy, the most revolting and oppressive with which the earth was ever cursed or man debased, we will co-operate and be known as 'Republicans' until the contest be terminated."

According to historians, it was Horace Greeley who had urged the Michigan leaders to adopt the name Republican. But a former Vermonter, Jacob Merritt Howard, the first Whig Congressman from Michigan and later a Senator, drafted the resolutions passed. Some regarded him as "The Godfather of the Republican Party." Shaftsbury, Vermont, has erected a sign in his honor.

The United States Department of the Interior has honored Jackson with a landmark to commemorate where this first Republican state convention was held, "under the oaks," in 1854. As recently as July 6, 1994, the Associated Press notes in a syndicated column, *Today In History:* "In 1854, the Republican Party came into being at a convention in Jackson, Michigan."

Cartoon of Horace Greeley from Harper's *NH Profiles*

THE REPUBLICAN PARTY

Congressman Amos Tuck Said to Have

Suggested the Name in 1852.

[Boston Globe.]

Washington dispatches announce that on July 6 the republican party will celebrate the fiftieth anniversary of its birth at Jackson, Mich.

With greater propriety the celebration might have been held in Exeter, N. H., October 12, 1903, for it is a fact that the republican party received its name in Exeter, October 12, 1853, by the late Amos Tuck, once Lincoln's colleague in congress and his personal friend.

In 1847 there were in New Hampshire five political parties, the democratic, which had long controlled the state, and opposed to that the whig, the abolition, the free soil, and the independent democratic parties, the last led by George G. Fogg, John P. Hale and Amos Tuck. The four minority parties united in opposition to the democratic, and in the election of March, 1847, carried the legislature by a majority of three. There was no election of governor, and at the organization of the legislature in June that body elected John P. Hale speaker and General Anthony Colby, a whig, governor. John P. Hale was soon elected to the national senate, and by a fusion of the minority parties in the First district Amos Tuck was elected to congress and twice re-elected.

The several minority parties had maintained their individual organizations, and in 1853 it became apparent that steps must be taken to weld them in a more perfect union. This feeling was especially strong in Rockingham county. Late in September, 1853, Amos Tuck sent to a few leaders letters of the following import:

"We deem it advisable to hold an informal meeting composed of some of the principal members of the parties at this place on October 12, at Major Blake's hotel. One of the principal objects of this informal meeting is to fix on a plan of harmonizing the different party organizations, whereby a more united co-operation can be secured, and the four parties may pull together under one title of organization."

The meeting was held at the appointed time, with an attendance of fourteen. No record of the meeting was kept, and no publicity was given to its proceedings at the time. The last survivor of the fourteen attendants was the late D. Homer Batchelder, then of Londonderry, who, on August 10, 1887, being then a a resident of Danversport, Mass., published an extended report of the meeting.

Its attendants included John P. Hale, Mr. Tuck, Ichabod Bartlett, Asa McFarland, George G. Fogg and others of less fame. At this meeting, to quote from Mr. Batchelder's report, Mr. Tuck "proposed that we use our influence to the end that all political organizations which had rather informally acted together thus far in behalf of one general object should drop individual titles and hereafter be known and recognized as one party under one common title, and that the name republican be prefixed to the party, and that it be hereafter known as the republican party."

Mr. Tuck argued that "this name would seem to convey its principles, and would be more likely to become nationalized, take on canonical respectability and be significant of a great national party in process of time." Attendants at the meeting agreed to use their individual influence to effect the result suggested by Mr. Tuck. Early in 1854 the republican had become a recognized party name in this section, and the honor of its suggestion and practical application is the sole right of Amos Tuck.

The Boston Globe, 1904

OTHER CLAIMS

The Michigan convention was followed shortly thereafter by a series of other Republican state conventions.

Most historians refer to A. N. Cole, publisher of *The Genesee Valley Free Press,* who participated in an earlier convention at Friendship, New York, in May of 1854. Cole claimed that Horace Greeley had named the party 'Republican' in a letter to Cole and Cole published it in his newspaper before the convention. Cole is said to have changed his masthead to recognize the new party and considered his paper to be "the pioneer Republican Journal of America." Current historians have been unable to locate a copy of this paper.

Other noteworthy 1854 conventions were also held in Iowa, Maine, Ohio, Vermont and Massachusetts where the name Republican was formally accepted. Still none of the claims from those states has received widespread recognition or been considered superior to Ripon, Jackson—or Exeter. In fact, Amos Tuck was successful in dispelling the Massachusetts claim with his speech at Downer's Landing in 1878.

Thus, it should be noted that **every known recorded claim for the birthplace of the Republican party, except New Hampshire's, took place sometime during the calendar year of 1854. The Exeter meeting was clearly recorded as having taken place in 1853.**

THEY ALL CLAIM...

**BUT
IT
STARTED
HERE**

A Summary of Historical Research on Amos Tuck and the Birthplace of the Republican Party at Exeter, New Hampshire

HISTORIANS DISAGREE

The controversy appears to circle around what actually constitutes the "founding" as compared to the beginning, origin or "birthplace" of the party. According to *The American Heritage Dictionary of the English Language,* a birthplace is "the place where something originates." Founding is defined: "to bring something into existence and set it in operation."

"The Republican party, though born in Wisconsin, was conceived and named at a meeting in Exeter, NH, called by Amos Tuck in 1853," according to Ronald and Grace Jager in *History of the Granite State.*

Most historians, in determining the birthplace or founding of the Republican party, reach one of two conclusions: one group contends it took place at either Ripon, Wisconsin, or Jackson, Michigan; the second group gives Exeter, New Hampshire, the credit.

There follows a listing of representative historians from both groups from whom material has been obtained in preparing this report.

Historians Favoring Ripon or Jackson in 1854

- Henry Wilson: *Rise and Fall of Slave Power in America,* 1874
- Western Historical Society (Butterfield): *History of Fond du Lac County,* 1880
- Frank A. Flower: *History of the Republican Party,* 1884
- Stephen M.: *Slavery and Freedom,* 1888

- James Ford Rhodes: *History of the United States Compromise of 1850,* 1893
- J. A. Woodburn: *Political Parties and Party Problems,* 1903
- Francis Curtis: *The Republican Party,* 1904
- A. F. Gilman: *The Origin of the Republican Party,* 1914
- Samuel M. Pedrick: *The Life of Alvan E. Bovay,* 1915
- Frank Hendrick: *Republicanism of Nineteen-Twenty,* 1920
- Frederick J. Blue: *The Free Soilers—Third Party Politics 1848–1854,* 1923
- Don C. Seitz: *Horace Greeley Founder of New York Tribune,* 1926
- William Starr Meyers: *The Republican Party—A History,* 1928
- Wilfred E. Binkley: *American Political Parties, Their Natural History,* 1959
- Andrew Wallace Crandall: *The Early History of the Republican Party 1854–56,* 1960
- Wayne Andrews: *Concise Dictionary of American History,* 1967
- George H. Mayer: *The Republican Party, 1854–1966,* 1967
- Hans L. Trefousse: *The Republican Party 1854–1864,* 1973
- Fred Schwengel: *The Republican Party,* 1987
- William E. Gienapp: *The Origins of the Republican Party 1852–1856,* 1987

Most of the historians in the foregoing group refer to both Ripon and Jackson, make comparisons between the claims of the two communities, and then select one town over the other. None of the writers who selected either Ripon or Jackson ever mentions Exeter.

Since Exeter was not considered by these historians, it must be assumed that none of them had learned of what had occurred in New Hampshire in 1853. Otherwise, they would have discussed it.

There was one Wisconsin historian, perhaps the only one, who knew what took place at Exeter and also had "personal knowledge" of the Ripon meetings. In an article published on April 2, 1898, in the *Wisconsin State Register* A. J. Turner repudiated the Ripon claim:

> The Republican party did not have its conception, birth, or baptism at Ripon, March 20, 1854, or at any other time, and it was not christened by Hon. A. E. Bovay.

He added:

> ...years ago, Exeter, N.H., put in its claim for primacy, which, so far as I know, has never been controverted.

Thus, he concluded:

> **The earliest steps for the formation of the Republican party were taken at the private conference at Exeter, N. H., Oct. 12, 1853...at which a new party organization to be called 'Republican' was decided upon and the machinery set in motion to effect it.**

HISTORIANS FAVORING EXETER IN 1853

- Rev. George E. Street: *Amos Tuck, A Memorial Discourse*, 1879
- Jeremiah W. Dearborn: *Sketch of the Life and Character of Hon. Amos Tuck*, 1888
- A. J. Turner: *Genesis of the Republican Party*, 1898
- Charles Robert Corning: *Amos Tuck*, 1902
- James O. Lyford: *Life of Edward Rollins*, 1906
- Jonathan Eastman Pecker papers (1833–1912): *George G. Fogg, Biographical Sketch*
- Stearns, Ezra S., Ed., *Genealogical & Family History of the State of N.H.*, 1908
- Everett S. Stackpole: *History of New Hampshire*, 1916
- Hobart Pillsbury: *New Hampshire, A History*, 1927
- Elwin L. Page: *Abraham Lincoln in New Hampshire*, 1929
- American Council of Learned Societies: *Dictionary of American Biography*, 1936
- Edward J. Parshley: *New Hampshire—A Historical Sketch*, 1938
- Dudley P. Frasier: *The Antecedents & Formation of the Republican Party in New Hampshire 1845–1860*, 1947
- Russell P. Burbank: *Exeter, The Birthplace of the Republican Party*, 1954
- Malcolm Moos: *The Republicans—A History of Their Party*, 1956
- J. Duane Squires: *The Granite State of the United States*, 1956
- William H. Mandrey: *Republican Party Named at Exeter*, 1958
- Philip M. Marston: *Amos Tuck and the Beginning in w Hampshire of the Republican Party*, 1960
- Richard H. Sewell: *John P. Hale and the Politics of Abolition*, 1965

- Thomas R. Bright: *The Emergence of the Republican Party in New Hampshire 1853–1857*, 1972
- Ronald & Grace Jager: *History of the Granite State,* 1983
- Steven Paul McGiffen: *Prelude to Republicanism: Issues in the Development of Political Parties in New Hampshire, 1835–1847*, 1984
- Franklin Brooks: *The Education of a New Hampshire Philanthropist,* 1992

Historians have usually overlooked New Hampshire's role in the establishment of the Republican party. Almost every schoolboy is familiar with the facts of the meetings in Ripon, Wisconsin, and in Jackson, Michigan, held respectively on March 20 and July 6, 1854. Few, even among professional students of the matter, however, seem to be aware of New Hampshire's precedence over both these mid-Western states.

"Yet the facts are clear enough, and are well worth recording…. Thus, months before either the Ripon meeting or the assembly at Jackson, New Hampshire men pioneered in the formation of a new political group to oppose the Democrats. Moreover, they hit upon the very name which was later accepted, and which has now endured for more than a century."
—*J. Duane Squires, Ph.D., New Hampshire state historian, in The Granite State of the United States, Vol. 1 (1956).*

In September, 1853, he (Tuck) called a meeting at Exeter of the forces gathering to resist Slavery, at which he suggested that the name 'Republican' be given to the new party. This antedated by several months the mass meeting held in Ripon, Wisconsin, that adopted the same name.
—*From the Diary & Correspondence of Benjamin Brown French, as edited by his grandson, Amos Tuck French, 1904.*

Amos Tuck French (1863–1941) was the son of Amos' daughter Ellen and Francis O. French. Like his father, he was a successful banker, serving as the director of the Manhattan Trust Co., 1893–1908.

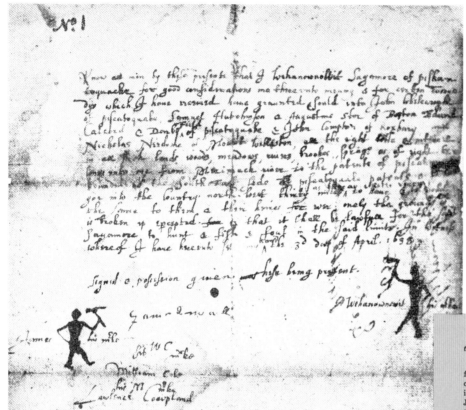

Deed from Totems of Indian Sagamores to Rev. John Wheelwright *Exeter Historical Society*

The following transcription of the deed is taken from Charles H. Bell's *History of the Town of Exeter:*

Know all men by these presents that I Wehanownowit Sagamore of piskatoquacke for good considerations me therevnto mouing & for certen comodys which I have received have graunted & sould vnto John Whelewright of piscatoquake, Samuel Hutchinson & Augustine Stor of Boston Edward Calcord & Darby Field of piscatoquake & John Compton of Roxbury and Nicholas Needome of Mount Walliston all the right title & interest in all such lands, woods, meadows, riuers, brookes springs as of right belong vnto me from Merimack riuer to the patents of piscatoquake bounded wch the South East side of piscatoquake patents & so to goe into the Country north West thirty miles as far as oyster riuer to haue & to hold the same to them & their heires forever, onely the ground wh is broken up excepted. & that it shall be lawfull for the said Sagamore to hunt & fish & foul in the said limits. In Witness whereof I haue herevnto set my hand the 3d day of April 1638.

Signed & possession giuen.   These being present

James Wall.
James   his m'ke   Wehanownowit   his m'ke.

   his W. C. m'ke.
William Cole

   his M m'ke.
Lawrence Cowpland

EXETER (1995 POPULATION 13,000) COMMEMORATES THE BIRTHPLACE OF THE REPUBLICAN PARTY

It was not until October 1993's *Associated Press* story, written by Frank Baker, that Ripon became aware of Exeter's claim as the true birthplace of the Republican Party.

The news came at a bad time for the Wisconsin community. Its place in the 1994 edition of the *Guinness Book of World Records* for producing the world's largest cookie was being oppugned by a California shopping center. The Ripon bakers were disparaging the challenge by pointing out that the west-coast entry was baked in separate pieces, held together by a topping of chocolate icing. This was not legitimate competition for the dairy state's record-setting one-piece, 907.9 square foot, 3,500 lb. inch-thick tidbit containing 3,839,207 chocolate chips. The local paper said the California imposter reminded them of "a guy who stuck a feather in his cap and called it macaroni."

In responding to Exeter's claim, the Ripon paper further editorialized:

> "Hey, where have those people been? Like 150 years of silence? C'mon! Are they just now waking up like Rip (or is it Ripon?) Van Winkle and figuring out a new way to make a tourist buck? Is the profile and attraction of the Old Man of the Mountain on Profile Mountain wearing off?...Exeter's claimant, a Democrat in Washington named Amos Tuck, was thinking about a new party. He was head of the New England tourist bureau and simply expressed his viewpoint at a public meeting. 'I wish we could try something new,' he was heard to exclaim. But his friends were not excited, they said, 'Why fix it, if it ain't broke?' Tuck went out and drank heavily at the local tavern. That was it.... Besides, Exeter sounds utterly too British.

It's unlikely that the stalwart sons of Exeter who joined the patriots at Bunker Hill were ever "too" British. As John L. Hayes said in his published speech of February 7, 1845: "She (New Hampshire) sacrificed more of her blood and treasure in the war of the Revolution than any other state." Contrast Exeter's history with the irony that Ripon's lineage came from Yorkshire!

In 1638, Exeter was settled by Reverend John Wheelwright and others on land purchased from the Indians, known by them as Piscatoquake. It was one of the first four towns established in New Hampshire and served as the state's capital during the Revolutionary War. At that time the township exceeded 500 square miles. Today it occupies less than 17.

On July 21, 1774, a Provincial Congress began meeting in Exeter. This body served as the de facto government of New Hampshire. Desiring to be formally recognized, this Provincial Congress petitioned the Continental Congress, meeting in Philadelphia, for legitimacy. On December 21, 1775, the Continental Congress recommended New Hampshire be the first of the thirteen colonies to establish a government "of the people."

Accordingly, in Exeter on January 5, 1776, New Hampshire's Fifth Provincial Congress adopted America's first people's Constitution. It anteceded by seven months the national Declaration of Independence which was not signed by members of the Continental Congress until July 4th—another great historic first both for Exeter and New Hampshire.

A Summary of Historical Research on Amos Tuck and the Birthplace of the Republican Party at Exeter, New Hampshire

Still preserved by the American Independence Museum at Exeter are original printings of the United States Constitution and Declaration of Independence.

In 1859 *The American Ballot and Rockingham County Intelligencer* newspaper moved from Portsmouth to Exeter because "Portsmouth is in the extreme corner of the state, nearly surrounded by salt water. Exeter is in the heart of the county with prosperous and flourishing towns adjoining it on every hand, the county offices are here, and the town is in fact the business center of the community."

Amos Tuck served as a trustee of the Robinson Female Seminary which was founded in 1869 at Exeter. Tuck had assisted in finding the land and the architect for the school. In those days when the concept of equal education for the sexes was new, benefactor William Robinson wanted the "Seminary to do for girls what the Phillips Academy does for boys."

Exeter in 1860 *Exeter Historical Society*

Dictionary of American Biography: "Tuck's fine appearance, personal charm, and public spirit gave him a prominent place in that group of lawyers and party leaders which made Exeter one of the influential centers of New England life in the nineteenth century."

Thus, it seems particularly appropriate that one of the two great national political parties of today should also have been born in this town—a distinction further embellished by the political significance of New Hampshire's "First-in-the-Nation" presidential primary which has commanded the country's respect since 1920.

COMMEMORATIVE PLAQUE UNVEILED IN 1929

On September 26, 1929, at Exeter a ceremony was held by the Rockingham County Republican Club in connection with the unveiling of a bronze tablet which had been placed on the Squamscot House (formerly Blake's Hotel). The tablet read: "On this site, the Republican Party was first so named by Amos Tuck, October 12, 1853." It remains there today, upon the same building, now re-named "Blake's Hotel."

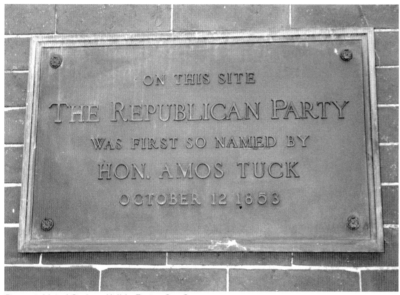

Bronze tablet of Gorham Hall in Exeter *Cay Gregg*

The keynote address at the event was delivered by Albertus T. Dudley who recounted the details of the October 12, 1853, meeting and its objective:

> to fix on a plan for harmonizing the different party organizations, whereby a more united co-operation can be secured and the four parties can pull together under one title of organization.

He continued:

> Now the year 1854 is usually called the birth-year of the Republican party. As many are the states that claim to be the birth-place as were the cities of old which claimed Homer.

> The fact seems to be that the party burst into life in many places at the same time, when the conditions became ripe, as a flame sometimes breaks forth on a log, as it smoulders in the fireplace, here and there over its entire length. The question which we should seek to answer is therefore not when and where the first formal convention was held, but where and through whom came the first suggestion of the Republican party which should emerge from the disintegration of the parties of the past.

> A great amount of preparatory work had to be done during the ten years preceding 1856 (the first Republican National Convention) to break down the bars of prejudice and self-seeking among politicians, and bring about the amalgamation that was the Republican party. Mr. Tuck stood in the very forefront of this activity.

> So it happened that when Amos Tuck returned to private life in 1853 he was the natural leader of those who saw no hope except in a new political organization.

Amos Tuck must be considered not alone one of the important founders of the Republican Party, but the first prophet to herald its coming.

101ST ANNIVERSARY CELEBRATED IN 1954

On October 22, 1954, during the administration of Governor Hugh Gregg, the state again honored Exeter and Amos Tuck at the Town Hall, celebrating the 101st Anniversary of the party's birth.

The *Exeter News-Letter* remarked:

Exeter can point with pride to the fact that the groundwork for the formation of one of the two great political parties of the nation was undertaken here.

The Exeter High School band played outside. Inside, the hall was jammed. Every major elected office holder and Republican party official shared the stage. The event was capped by the serving of a giant multi-tiered birthday cake enjoyed by 500 jubilant participants.

Gregg said the spirit was somewhat reminiscent of another Republican rally held in the same town hall over a century earlier, exuberantly described in Benjamin Gerrish, Jr.'s journals: "Amos Tuck called the meeting to order and introduced the speaker....Cheer upon cheer arose, hats and handkerchiefs were waved in the air, the Band played a lively tune, and the wildest enthusiasm prevailed."

**101st Anniversary
of the Founding of
The Republican Party**

**Program
October 22, 1954**

7:00 - 7:45 P. M. —— At Bandstand
Concert by Exeter High School Band

8:00 P. M. —— At Exeter Town Hall
Invocation Rev. Frederick A. Champion, Rye, N. H.
Singing of "America"
Introduction of Honored Guests by William W. Treat,
Chairman New Hampshire Republican State Committee

Including
United States Senator Robert W. Upton
United States Representative Chester E. Merrow
United States Representative Norris Cotton
Honorable Lane Dwinell,
President, New Hampshire Senate

State Welcome by Governor Hugh Gregg
and introduction of
United States Senator Styles Bridges,
President Pro Tempore
Introduction of Guest Speaker and Welcome
by United States Senator Styles Bridges

Guest Speaker
Honorable William A. Purtell,
United States Senator from Connecticut

Reception and Refreshments in the Town Hall for Guests
following the program

140TH ANNIVERSARY CELEBRATED IN 1993

On October 12, 1993, The New Hampshire Federation of Republican Women gave further recognition to the founding of the GOP, on the 140th anniversary of the Exeter meeting. In a ceremony at the Republican Party state headquarters in Concord, they presented a commemorative booklet describing its founding. It was accepted on behalf of the party by New Hampshire Governor Stephen Merrill. Remarks in support of the Exeter event were made by Senator Richard Lugar of Indiana who said he was delighted to have had "a chance to visit the real founding site."

It is an unfortunate historical gaffe that both the communities of Ripon, Wisconsin, and Jackson, Michigan, should have been honored by being declared national historic sites for their roles in the development of the Republican Party, whereas Exeter, New Hampshire, the real home of the Republican Party, has been ignored by so many historians.

Birthday cake enjoyed at 140th anniversary

A COMMEMORATIVE OF THE 140TH BIRTHDAY OF THE REPUBLICAN PARTY

This engraving, circa 1840, of Front Street, Exeter, New Hampshire, locates the site of Major Blake's Hotel, the birthplace of the Republican Party, October 12, 1853.
— Courtesy of the Exeter Historical Society.

Cover of 140th Birthday Commemorative Booklet provided by NH Federation of Republican Women

1994: RECOGNITION BY THE NEW HAMPSHIRE REPUBLICAN PARTY

The New Hampshire Republican Party included the following statement in its 1994 Platform:

> **New Hampshire is proud to be the birthplace of the Republican Party, which was established at a meeting convened by Amos Tuck in Exeter on October 12, 1853. We reaffirm our first-in-the-nation presidential primary as the best test of whether someone should serve in the highest office of the land.**

In 1995, presidential candidates in New Hampshire's first-in-the-nation primary announced their candidacies at Exeter.

Senators Bob Dole and Arlen Specter, both members of the Amos Tuck Society, chose the Exeter Town Hall as the place to announce their presidential ambitions. They had selected the site because of Exeter's role in the birth of the Republican party and its proximity to the structure which had been known as Blake's Hotel.

On March 31st, Senator Specter spoke to his supporters within the Town Hall. Two weeks later, Senator Dole addressed a crowd of 2,500 from its front steps. Before extensive national media coverage, the two Senators made reference to Amos Tuck's leadership in establishing the GOP's birthplace. Lamar Alexander also gave similar credit when addressing the Exeter Chamber of Commerce.

On April 14th, Congressman Bob Dornan chose to make his presidential announcement both on the steps of Blake's Hotel (Gorham Hall) and across the street on the steps of the Congregational Church where Tuck held his first meeting in 1845. Dornan related Amos Tuck's concern with slavery in the early 1840s to current issues of the day and the significance of adhering to Republican principles.

As the *Laconia Citizen* commented editorially, "The symbolism of announcing in Exeter is proving too enticing for Republicans to resist." All of this interest by national candidates to recognize Exeter as the true birthplace of the Republican party was generated by the Amos Tuck Society which was formed in 1994.

Entrance to Gorham Hall adorned for Dornan announcement
Cay Gregg

The Exeter News-Letter *Reprinted with permission of the Exeter News-Letter*

A Summary of Historical Research on Amos Tuck and the Birthplace of the Republican Party at Exeter, New Hampshire

1995: GRAND CELEBRATION OF GOP'S 142ND BIRTHDAY

The Amos Tuck Society (see page 89) arranged a major commemoration of the 142nd birthday of the founding of the Republican Party in New Hampshire on October 12, 1995.

In conjunction with its second annual meeting, the Society was funded by Tyco International, Ltd. of Exeter to celebrate the historic occasion. The Society commissioned distinguished New Hampshire playwright Dr. Paul Mroczka to write an original play, *The Well Font — The Story of Tuck,* for its world premiere at the Exeter Town Hall where Tuck's good friend, Abraham Lincoln, had addressed the townspeople in 1860.

The play tells the story of Amos Tuck and his leadership in the conception of Republicanism. This professional presentation, videotaped for subsequent distribution, defines the historical accuracy of the role both Tuck and Exeter played in the origin of the Republican Party.

As part of the evening program, 1996 Republican and Democratic presidential candidates were invited to participate in a "synchronized amble" from the Tuck homestead at 89 Front Street to the Town Hall, carrying political signs of the period and accompanied by musicians playing the instruments and tunes of the 1850s.

Vintage dress and horse-drawn carriages of the period were designed to enrich the ambiance. A non-partisan event, it was foreseen as an historical first for Exeter, New Hampshire, and the nation.

The Exeter Brass Band, formed in 1847 when Amos Tuck was active in the community, was included in the program where they traditionally play, in the Swasey Pavilion, a small bandstand directly in front of the Town Hall. The pavilion "is the work of eminent architect, Henry Bacon, who was influenced in his design by Daniel Chester French. These men are best remembered for their collaboration on the Lincoln Memorial in Washington, D.C." (From a June 1971 *NH Profiles* article written by historians James L. Garvin and Nancy Merrill.)

Swasey Pavilion *Exeter Historical Society*

CONTENTION

Slavery: the Polarizing Issue

The Republican party of Lincoln was formed in the mid-nineteenth century when the Democrats, in control of the White House, were tolerant of slavery. The emergence of a new political fusion which came to be known as Republican was fueled by voters in the northern states who were generally committed to abolition. Thus, the true beginning of the Republican party should be traced to the earliest public remonstration over an issue of such importance that it would result in the Civil War.

It was Amos Tuck and John P. Hale who, in a call signed by 263 other Democrats, held a convention in Exeter on February 22, 1845, to express their indignation over the slavery issue. The call for their meeting (seven years ahead of the Ripon meetings) stated in part:

> Believing that the present scheme of (the) annexation (of Texas) is in violation of the fundamental principles of Democracy, the doctrine of States rights, strict construction of the Constitution, and regard for equal rights, and wishing to raise our voices against a scheme which will tend to extend and perpetuate slavery, and to weaken the influence of free representation in Congress...

The principles declared in the resolutions passed at that 1845 gathering were exactly the same as those that would become the basis of the Republican platform adopted at the first Republican National Convention in Philadelphia in 1856, which formally initiated the party of Lincoln.

This re-adoption of principles did not occur by coincidence. It was Amos Tuck who had originally assisted in their formulation at his 1845 meeting, then participated in their incorporation as a vice president of the national convention in 1856.

Note the similarity between the resolutions:

From the minutes of the 1845 convention at Exeter:

> "Resolved: That a direct or indirect advocacy of slavery, or support of those measures which will foster and encourage it, is wholly inconsistent with the doctrines of human equality and universal justice, and that nothing but the restraints of the Constitution, and a regard for the stability of the present Union of the States, should withhold the people of a free State from denouncing an institution which disgraces our Republic in the eyes of the whole civilized world."

From the minutes of the 1856 convention at Philadelphia:

> "Resolved: That the Constitution confers upon Congress sovereign power over the Territories of the United States for their government; and that in the exercise of this power, it is both the right and the imperative duty of Congress to prohibit in the Territories those twin relics of barbarism—Polygamy and Slavery."

John P. Hale, one of the most exhilarating speakers to address the Philadelphia convention said:

> "I have just come from New Hampshire. They talk to you here, perhaps, about the preferences of the different states. We had no preferences there. We were for the cause—we were for liberty—we were for the great principles of the Constitution carried out faithfully, and no matter who might be the standard-bearer, we were the soldiers to the cause, and we were ready to fight under any true man." (Proceedings: First Republican Nominating Convention in Philadelphia, 1856)

Slavery was the issue upon which both sets of resolutions were drawn; thus, in 1845, Tuck and Hale were precursors in publicly decrying its expansion. When elected in 1847, Hale was the first abolitionist in the United States Senate and Tuck was one of only three United States Congressmen with the same sentiment.

It should be noted that even at the subsequent 1860 Chicago Republican convention, when **Amos Tuck was a member of the Committee on Resolutions and Platform,** the following resolution was adopted:

> Resolved: That the new dogma that the Constitution, of its own force, carries slavery into any or all of the territories of the United States, is a dangerous political heresy, at variance with the explicit provisions of that instrument itself, with contemporaneous exposition, and with legislative and judicial precedent; is revolutionary in its tendency, and subversive to the peace and harmony of the country.

Again, the profound influence of Committeeman Amos Tuck had been officially recorded.

Tuck Fights Texas and Kansas-Nebraska

Tuck and Hale's public posture as abolitionists in 1845 had been provoked by the annexation of Texas.

The *Exeter Newsletter* of February 24, 1845, in reporting the meeting at the Congregational Church two days earlier said:

> As to Texas, the speakers were generally willing to receive her into the Republican fold, if she might come in constitutionally, & upon republican principles; but they could not recognize that as a Republican form of Government, within the meaning of the Constitution, which trampled on the rights of man, and deprived one half of the whole population of all civil rights and civil liberty. [Editor's Note: Use of the words "Republican" and "republican principles" by the reporter, even at that early date.]

But by 1854, Texas had been admitted to the Union and the same fight had progressed to aggressive opposition of the Kansas-Nebraska bill. Tuck had joined that fight also.

In a letter to the Hon. I. Washburn, Jr., dated February 24, 1854, Tuck spoke of the "greatest treason of the age," alluding to President Pierce and his support of the Nebraska bill. "Assure our friends," wrote Tuck, "that the number is increasing daily in this State, who appreciate the serious responsibility, on us, who have furnished the man in the executive chair, to strike a death blow to the treason, which that man is conspiring to perpetuate." (Historian Elwin Page found this letter in Maine.)

But both meetings in Ripon, along with subsequent conventions held in Wisconsin, Michigan, and other states, were not convened to address the slavery issue until 1854 when the Nebraska bill was their concern.

The call for the first Ripon meeting as published February 29, 1854, in the *Ripon Herald* read:

> NEBRASKA. A meeting will be held at 6 1/2 o'clock this (Wednesday) evening in the Congregational Church to remonstrate against the Nebraska swindle.

The call for the second Ripon meeting as published March 15, 1854, in the *Ripon Herald* read:

> THE NEBRASKA BILL. A bill expressly intended to extend the institution of slavery has passed the Senate by a very large majority, many northern senators voting for it and many more sitting in their seats and not voting at all. It is evidently destined to pass the House and become a law unless its progress is arrested by the general uprising of the North against it.
>
> THEREFORE, we the undersigned, believing this community to be nearly or quite unanimously in opposition to the nefarious scheme, would call a public meeting of citizens of all parties at the school house in Ripon, on Monday evening, March 20, at 6:30 o'clock, to resolve petition and to organize against it." (Signed by A. E. Bovay and fifty-three others)

Historian Francis Curtis was uninformed when he wrote:

> At these two meetings (in Ripon) was started the earliest systematic work begun anywhere in the country to bring about the coalition of the enemies of slavery extension, who were eventually fused into a homogeneous and aggressive party, adopting the name Republican.

Slavery had previously motivated the forming of New Hampshire's Independent Democrats by Tuck in 1845.

It Resulted in a New Political Party

In his biography of Alvan Bovay, Samuel M. Pedrick said "Bovay was possessed with sufficient sagacity to read the signs of the times and to predict that a new political party would soon be formed which would become national in its scope and character." Neither Pedrick nor Bovay was aware this had already taken place at Exeter in 1845.

In 1845, Tuck had the foresight and courage to separate from the Democrats and establish a new political party in the state. In his autobiography Tuck quoted the *New Hampshire Patriot*, the journal of the Democratic party, as saying at that time "The Democratic Party will teach Amos Tuck, John L. Hayes and N. P. Cram, that it can do better without them than with them."

Dr. Andrew Preston Peabody, a renowned clergyman, said,

> I well remember the utter hopelessness with which the great public viewed this little band of Independents in New Hampshire. They were thought to have destroyed their political future beyond all retrieve.

In a letter dated June 2, 1847, Tuck wrote to Whig leader Asa Fowler, Esq., referring to the confusion being created by the

> Pierces and Athertons and Norrises of New Hampshire, and all other despicable politicians, whose patriotism is made up of unmitigated selfishness, and whose ambition is pure vanity. God be thanked, that the thread of my connection with a party cursed by such leaders, is fully severed.

Although its members called the new fusion "Independent Democrats" Tuck subsequently succeeded in pioneering the founding of its successor party which he named "Republican."

Franklin Brooks, in his extensive review of the Amos and Edward Tuck papers, wrote: "After the repeal of the Missouri Compromise, Tuck led his Independent Democrats into the new Republican party."

By the time of the meeting at Blake's Hotel there were four major parties, all opposed to the extension of slavery. Amos Tuck's Exeter meeting on October 12, 1853, was the earliest recorded gathering of substantial political leaders assembled for the purpose of continuing the party he had created and proposed to name it Republican.

The enduring significance of what Tuck had achieved was perhaps best recorded by an editorial in the *Exeter News-Letter* at the time of his death which read: "Four millions of slaves were made freemen as the result of that little meeting at the court house (First Congregational Church) in Exeter on an inclement day in the winter of 1845."

Tuck's call for the 1853 meeting had been clear: "One of the principal objects of this informal meeting is to fix on a plan of harmonizing the different party organizations, whereby a more united co-operation can be secured and the four parties may pull together under one title of organization."

In further authenticating his intent, Tuck later recalled, both in his series of articles published by the *Exeter News-Letter* in 1876

and in his speech at Downer's Landing in 1878, that he was talking Republican principles as far back as the Exeter convention in 1845.

On September 15, 1876 he had written in the *Exeter News-Letter* that even his Independent Democrat had "advocated Republicanism for eleven years before the Republican party came into being."

In a letter to his friend, George Fogg, dated March 14, 1876, Tuck wrote: "New Hampshire was saved from their democracy in 1845--46, by the aggregate honesty, wisdom, devotion, patriotism of the people, not even Lincoln being able to claim much more than that he followed the inspiration to action manifested by the people."

New Hampshire's Claim Could Conceivably Go Back to 1845.

Thus, instead of designating Blake's Hotel as the birthplace of the Republican party, New Hampshire could reach even farther back in claiming that it was actually born across the street in Exeter at the First Congregational Church seven years earlier.

It was a massive public meeting to condemn slavery and form the new party.

The fact that the initial name of "Independent Democrat" was later changed to Republican, at Tuck's suggestion, does not alter the truth that it was all part of Tuck's original concept. Though he retroactively identified his Independent Democrat party as Republican, Tuck is indisputably the father of the Republican party which was New Hampshire-born in 1845. Unfortunately, historians did not acknowledge Tuck's paternity until the second Exeter meeting in 1853.

AMOS TUCK SOCIETY

Amos Tuck of Exeter had both the vision and leadership to conceive a new political party based upon the principles he established, which have endured for over 150 years. It was in Exeter's Town Hall, built at Tuck's behest and still standing today, that his friend and the party's first president, Abraham Lincoln, addressed the voters of Exeter during the 1860 campaign. It marked the beginning of what became formally known as the Republican Party of Lincoln.

In 1994, in recognition of this extraordinary man who was the father of the Republican party and his incredible accomplishments, a non-profit, tax exempt association was formed and appropriately named the Amos Tuck Society. Its purpose is to share with the nation this unique place which New Hampshire deserves in American political history.

The Society is an educational, commemorative organization, whose goals include promoting the historical accuracy of the origin of the Republican party, its ideals, and the principles on which it was founded. It is not a political association.

The Society encourages research about the Republican Party, sponsors lectures and seminars, and publishes newsletters for its members. Annual meetings are held on October 12th of each year in Exeter. Tax-exempt charter membership at one hundred dollars is available and open to anyone interested in its mission.

It is the belief of the Amos Tuck Society Founders that by revisiting the real roots of the Grand Old Party, and by setting the chronological record straight on the Party's genesis, Amos Tuck and New Hampshire will be properly recognized.

For membership information contact the Society at Post Office Box #1853, Exeter, NH, 03833-1151. Telephone: 603/881-9184. FAX: 603/595-9010.

Bust of Amos Tuck by Daniel Chester French at New Hampshire State Library
R.P. Hale

BIBLIOGRAPHY

Books

American Council of Learned Societies. *Dictionary of American Biography.* Charles Scribner & Sons, 1936

Andrews, Wayne. *Concise Dictionary of American History.* Charles Scribner & Sons, N.Y., 1967

Angle, Paul M. *The Lincoln Reader.* Rutgers University Press, 1947

Barnes, William. *Origin and Early History of the Republican Party.* J. B. Lyon Co., Albany, N.Y., 1906

Bell, Charles H. *History of the Town of Exeter.* J.E. Farwell & Co. Boston, 1888

_____. *Bench and Bar of New Hampshire.* Houghton-Mifflin & Co, Boston, N.Y., 1894

Binkley, Wilfred E. *American Political Parties, Their Natural History.* Alfred A. Knopf, N.Y., 1959

Blue, Frederick J. *Free Soilers—Third Party Politics, 1848–1854.* University of Illinois Press, 1923

Burns, James MacGregor. *The Vineyard of Liberty.* Alfred A. Knopf, N.Y. 1982

Butterfield, Roger. *American Past, A History of the United States from Concord to the Great Society.* Simon Schuster, 1947

Butterfield. *History of Fond du Lac County.* Western Historical Society, 1880

Carruth, Gorton & Associates. *American Facts and Dates.* Thomas & Crowell Company, N.Y. 1972

Charlton, Edwin A., *New Hampshire As It Is.* Tracy & Co. Claremont, N.H., 1856

Chase, Benjamin. *History of Old Chester, From 1719 to 1869.* Auburn, N.H., 1869

Christner, Henry. *Tin Horns and Calico.* Henry Holt & Co., 1945

Cole, Donald B. *Jacksonian Democracy in New Hampshire, 1800–1851.* Harvard Press, 1970.

_____. and McDonough, John J. *Witness to the Young Republic, A Yankee's Journal 1828–1870.* University Press of New England, Hanover and London, 1988.

Corning, Charles Robert. *Amos Tuck.* News-Letter Press, 1902.

Crandall, Andrew Wallace. *The Early History of the Republican Party 1854–1856.* Peter Smith, Gloucester, Mass., 1960

Cresson, Margaret French. *Journey into Fame: The Life of Daniel Chester French.* Harvard University Press, 1947.

Curtis, Francis. *The Republican Party, 1854–1904.* G. P. Putnam's Sons, 1904.

Dearborn, Rev. Jeremiah Wadleigh. *Life and Character of Amos Tuck.* Parsonsfield, Maine, 1888

_____. *A History of the First Century of the Town of Parsonsfield, Maine.* Brown, Thurston & Co, Portland, Maine, 1888

Dow, Joseph. *Robert Tuck, of Hampton, New Hampshire, and His Descendants, 1638–1877.* David Clapp & Son, Boston, 1877

Flower, Frank A. *History of the Republican Party.* Union Publishing Co., Springfield, Ill., 1884

Foner, Eric. *Republican Party.* Oxford University Press, N.Y., 1970

French, Amos Tuck. *Diary and Correspondence of Benjamin Brown French.* New York, 1904

Gehner, R. F. *Origin of the Republican Party.* Ripon, Wisconsin 1931

Gienapp, William E. *Origins of the Republican Party.* Oxford University Press, 1986

Gilman, Prof. A.F. *Origin of the Republican Party.* Ripon College, July 1987

Goodman, Paul. *The Democratic-Republicans of Massachusetts.* Harvard University Press, 1964

Gordy, J.P. *Political History of the United States with Special Reference to the Growth of Political Parties.* N.Y., 1902

Hall, Benjamin F. *The Republican Party.* Miller, N.Y., 1856

Hayes, John L. A *Reminiscence of the Free-Soil Movement in New Hampshire, 1845.* Cambridge: John Wilson and Son, University Press, 1885

Hendrick, Frank, Ed. *Republicanism of Nineteen-Twenty.* Albany Evening Journal, the Journal Co., 1920

Holt, Michael F. *Political Crisis of the 1850s.* Wiley, N.Y., 1978

Howard, Jacob Merritt. *The Story of Shaftsbury, Vermont.* Farnhum & Farnhum, Shaftsbury, 1954

Isely, Jeter Allen. *Horace Greeley and the Republican Party, 1853–1861.* Princeton University Press, 1947

Jager, Ronald and Grace. *Government and People.* Winsor Publications, 1983

Knox, Thomas W. *The Republican Party and Its Leaders.* P. F. Collier, N.Y., 1892

Livingstone, William. *History of the Republican Party.* William Livingstone, Detroit, Michigan, 1900

Long, Hon. John Davis. *Republican Party: Its History, Principles and Policies.* William E. Smythe, Co., Boston, 1888

Lyford, James O. *Life of Edward Rollins.* Dana Estes & Co., 1906

MacKown, Alden Stuart. *Factionalism in the Republican Party.* University of Massachusetts, 1967

Mapes, David P. *History of Ripon and Its Founder.* Cramer, Aikens, & Cramer, Milwaukee, Wisconsin

Mayer, George H. *The Republican Party, 1854–1966.* Oxford University Press, N.Y., 1967

Miller, George H. *A History of Ripon, Wisconsin.* Worzalla Publishing Co., Stevenspoint, Wisconsin, 1964

Moos, Malcolm. *Republicans, A History of Their Party.* Random House, N.Y., 1956

Morison, Samuel Eliot. *The Oxford History of the American People.* Oxford University Press, N.Y., 1965

Murdock, Lily and Christopher Eck. *The Republican Heritage, A New Birth of Freedom.* Republican National Committee, 1994

Myers, William Starr. *The Republican Party—A History.* The Century Co., N.Y., London, 1928

Neely, Mark E., Jr. *The Abraham Lincoln Encyclopedia.* McGraw-Hill Book Company, 1982.

Nicolay, John A., and John Hay. *Complete Works of Abraham Lincoln.* The Century Co., N.Y., 1894

Page, Elwin L. *Abraham Lincoln in New Hampshire.* Houghton-Mifflin, 1929

Parker, Edward P. *History of Londonderry.* John D. Flagg, Andover, 1851

Parshley, Edward J. *New Hampshire: A Historical Sketch.* New Hampshire Planning & Development Commission, Concord, 1938

Pedrick, Samuel M. *The Life of Alvan Bovay.* Commonwealth Printers, Ripon, Wisconsin

_____. *The Republican Party's Origin.* Ripon Weekly Press, 1915

Pillsbury, Hobart. *New Hampshire: A History.* Lewis Historical Publishing Co., 1927

Potter, David M. *The Impending Crisis, 1848–1861.* Harper & Row, N.Y., 1976

Proceedings of the First Three Republican National Conventions of 1856, 1860, 1869. Charles W. Johnson, Minneapolis, 1893

Randall, Ruth Painter. *Lincoln's Sons.* Little, Brown & Co., 1955

Rhodes, Thomas Ford. *History of the United States Compromise of 1850.* 1893

Schlesinger, Arthur M., Jr. *History of United States Political Parties.* R.R. Bowker Co., N.Y., 1973

Schwengel, Fred. *The Republican Party, Its Heritage and History.* Acropolis Books Ltd., Washington, D.C., 1987

Seilhamer, George O. *History of the Republican Party.* Judge Publishing Co., N.Y., 1899

Seitz, Don C. *Horace Greeley, Founder of the New York Tribune.* Bobbs-Merrill Co., 1926

Sewell, Richard H. *John P. Hale and the Politics of Abolition.* Harvard University Press, 1965

Squires, J. Duane. *The Granite State of the United States.* American Historical Co., Inc., 1956

Stackpole, Everett S. *History of New Hampshire.* American Historical Society, N.Y., 1916

Stearns, Ezra A. *Genealogical and Family History of the State of New Hampshire.* Lewis Publishing Co., N.Y. and Chicago, 1908

Stoddard, Henry Luther. *Horace Greeley.* G.P. Putnam's Sons, 1946

Tuck, Amos. *Autobiographical Memoir of Amos Tuck.* Paris, Clarke and Bishop, 1902

White, Theodore A. *The Making of a President, 1964.* Atheneum Publishers, N.Y., 1961

Wilson, Henry. *The Rise and Fall of Slave Power in America.* Houghton-Mifflin, 1874

Woodburn, J. A. *Political Parties and Party Problems.* G.P. Putnam's Sons, N.Y. and London, 1903

Addresses, Articles, Collections

Allen, Stephen M. "Slavery and Freedom." Historical Addresses. Duxbury, MA 1888

Baldwin, Carolyn W. "The Dawn of the Republican Party in New Hampshire." *Historical New Hampshire,* Spring 1975

Bright, Thomas R. "The Emergence of the Republican Party in New Hampshire, 1853–1857." *Historical New Hampshire,* 1972

Brooks, Franklin. "Education of a New Hampshire Philanthropist." *Historical New Hampshire,* Summer/Spring 1992

_____. "The Lincoln Years in the Papers of Amos and Edward Tuck." *Dartmouth College Library Bulletin,* April 1981

Burbank, Russell P. "Birthplace of the Republican Party." *New Hampshire Profiles,* July 1954

Frasier, Dudley P. "The Antecedents and Formation of the Republican Party in New Hampshire, 1845–1860." (Paper, not dated)

Garvin, James. Address to Amos Tuck Society First Annual Meeting of 1994. Exeter, N. H.

Greeley, Horace. "Party Names and Public Duty." *New York Tribune,* June 1854.

Hall, Daniel. "Commemorative Addresses of John P. Hale and Abraham Lincoln." Delivered in Concord, 1892

Hayden, Thomas C. "Abraham Lincoln and the Formation of the Republican Party in New Hampshire." *Phillips-Exeter Academy Bulletin*, Winter 1983

Heffernan, Nancy Coffey and Ann Page Stecker. "New Hampshire Crosscurrents and Its Development." Tompson & Rutter Inc.,
        Grantham, N.H.

Leslies, Frank. *Popular Monthly Magazine.* January 1885

Mandrey, Dr. William H. "Republican Party Named at Exeter." *New Hampshire Sunday News,* Aug. 17, 1958

_____. "How the Republican Party Got Its Name." *New Hampshire Profiles*, July–August, 1972

Marston, Philip W. "Amos Tuck and the Beginning in New Hampshire of the Republican Party." *Historical New Hampshire,* Nov. 1960

McGiffen, Steven Paul. "Prelude to Republicanism: Issues in the Realignment of Political Parties in New Hampshire, 1835–1847." New Hampshire Historical Society

Pecker, Jonathan Eastman. *The Pecker Papers*. New Hampshire Historical Society

Phillips, Dr. Henry. "Political Parties in Exeter." Phillips-Exeter Academy

Republican National Committee. "Republican Platform of 1896." *National Party Platforms, Campaign of 1896*

Street, Rev. George E. "Eulogy on Amos Tuck." New Hampshire State Library, Jan. 11, 1880

Trefousse, Hans. "The Republican Party 1854–1864." *History of U.S. Political Parties*, A.M. Schlesinger, Ed., R.R. Bowker Co., 1973

Turner, Andrew J. "Genesis of the Republican Party." *Wisconsin State Register*, April 2, 1898

Papers and correspondence of Amos and Edward Tuck at the Baker Library at Darmouth. Papers and correspondence of Amos Tuck, Edward Tuck, John P. Hale, William H.Y. Hackett, Asa McFarland, William Plumer, Jr., James A. Young, John Preston, John Wentworth (1815–1888), George G. Fogg, Ichabod Bartlett, and David Currier at the New Hampshire Historical Society.

Appreciation to the New Hampshire Historical Society, the Exeter Historical Society, New Hampshire State Library, New Hampshire Department of State and Archives, Baker Library at Dartmouth, Phillips-Exeter Academy Library, the Portsmouth Athenaeum, American Antiquarian Society, Peabody Essex Museum, the Danvers Historical Society, New England Historic Genealogical Society; the Maine Historical Society, Biddeford, Maine Historical Society; Ripon Historical Society, The Little White School House; and the Library of Congress. Also, to the public libraries of Exeter, Manchester, Hudson, Nashua, Portsmouth, the Taylor Library in Londonderry, N.H.; Boston, Danvers, Salem, Peabody Institute Library, Mass.; Dyer-York Institute of Saco and the MacArthur Library of Biddeford, Maine; Milwaukee, Ripon, Ripon College Library and the Wisconsin State Library.

INDEX

PHOTO CREDITS